ASK THE BOFFINS *AGAIN!*

101 *More* Cool Answers To Weird Science Questions

PETER J. CLARK

ASK THE BOFFINS AGAIN!
101 MORE COOL ANSWERS TO
WEIRD SCIENCE QUESTIONS

ISBN: 9798390519752

DEDICATION

To my dear wife, *Christine*, without whose support

and cheering from the sidelines I'd have taken

many years to research and write this book!

TABLE OF CONTENTS

You're *still* curious after reading 'Ask The Boffins!'. You still want *more* answers about the world around you, but nobody seems to know exactly how things really work. This book gives you 101 more simple answers to weird and baffling questions about all sorts of things, in nature, the universe, and all kinds of clever science stuff!

Among the strange and wonderful things we've answered, you'll find out cool stuff like how many bubbles there are in a can of fizzy cola, can you lick your own elbow, do fish get sea-sick, how flowers know when to open and close, what makes farts and burps, whether the '5 second rule' for dropped food really is safe, whether AI machines could ever enslave humans, what pee's made of and if it's safe to drink, whether your fingernails still grow after you die ... and even what earthworms taste like!

For every weird question in this book, you'll get a simple answer first, then a proper explanation of the how and why. All the questions were chosen because most people don't know the real answers - but now *you* will! You'll be able to amaze your friends with more weird facts every day for months on end!

There are hours and hours of fun and learning to dig into here, and you'll end up being the smartest scientist you know.

1. WHY DO MAGPIES STEAL SHINY THINGS?

Magpies steal shiny objects due to their innate attraction to bright, reflective items, which they may use to impress potential mates or decorate their nests. Most birds build nests using twigs, grass, leaves, and other natural materials, which they collect from their surroundings.

Magpies are known for their tendency to collect and hoard shiny objects like jewelry, coins, and even cutlery. This behavior is thought to stem from their innate attraction to bright, reflective objects, which they perceive as valuable or useful in some way.

Some researchers believe that magpies may use these objects to impress potential mates or to decorate their nests, which can serve as a signal of their fitness and ability to acquire resources.

In contrast, most birds build their nests using natural materials that they find in their environment. This may include twigs, grass, leaves, and even mud or spider silk, depending on the species and location. Birds will typically collect these materials from nearby sources, such as trees, bushes, or the ground, and then use their beaks and claws to shape them into a nest.

The exact materials used and the construction process may vary depending on the species of bird and the location of the nest. For example, some birds may weave their nests into intricate shapes using long grasses, while others may create a simple depression in the ground or use existing cavities in trees or rocks.

The effectiveness of daily horoscopes is debatable, as they are typically based on vague and general predictions that can apply to a wide range of people. Horoscopes are based on the idea that the position of the stars and planets at the time of a person's birth can influence their personality and future events.

Daily horoscopes are a common feature of many newspapers, magazines, and websites, providing astrological predictions for people based on their zodiac sign. However, the effectiveness of horoscopes is a topic of debate, with many people skeptical of their accuracy and scientific validity.

One reason for this skepticism is that horoscopes tend to be based on vague and general predictions that could apply to almost anyone. For example, a horoscope might predict that someone will experience a change in their romantic life, which could be true for many people regardless of their zodiac sign or specific circumstances.

Horoscopes are based on the idea that the position of the stars and planets at the time of a person's birth can influence their personality and future events. This belief dates back thousands of years and is based on the principles of astrology, which attempts to interpret the influence of celestial bodies on human affairs.

However, the scientific validity of astrology and horoscopes is highly controversial, with many scientists and skeptics dismissing it as pseudoscience. They argue that there is no scientific evidence to support the idea that the position of the stars and planets at the time of a person's birth can have any meaningful influence on their personality or future events.

So, while some people may find horoscopes entertaining or insightful, their scientific validity and effectiveness remain highly questionable. The best way to approach horoscopes is with a healthy dose of skepticism and a recognition that they are not necessarily accurate or predictive of any particular outcome.

3. WHAT ARE THE ODDS OF INTELLIGENT LIFE ON OTHER PLANETS?

The probability of there being intelligent life on other planets in the universe is difficult to calculate due to the vastness of space and the unknown variables involved. Scientists use a statistical approach known as the Drake Equation to estimate the likelihood of finding extraterrestrial civilizations based on factors such as the number of habitable planets in the galaxy and the probability of life developing on them.

The question of whether there is intelligent life on other planets is a fascinating and longstanding topic of debate in the scientific community.

However, calculating the probability of finding such life is a complex and uncertain task, as there are many unknown variables involved.

To estimate the likelihood of finding intelligent life in the universe, scientists use a statistical approach known as the Drake Equation. This equation was developed by astronomer Frank Drake in 1961 and is based on a series of factors that can be used to estimate the number of communicative civilizations in our galaxy.

The Drake Equation includes factors such as the rate of star formation, the fraction of stars with planets, the number of habitable planets per star, the fraction of habitable planets that develop life, and the fraction of planets with life that develop intelligent civilizations capable of communication. It was developed by astronomer Frank Drake in 1961 as a way to formalize the factors involved in the search for extraterrestrial intelligence.

The equation takes into account a number of variables that are thought to affect the likelihood of finding intelligent life, such as the rate of star formation, the fraction of stars with planets, the number of habitable planets per star, the fraction of habitable planets that develop life, and the fraction of planets with life that develop intelligent civilizations capable of communication. The equation is expressed as:

$$N = R^* \times f\_p \times n\_e \times f\_l \times f\_i \times f\_c \times L$$

Where:

- N = the number of civilizations in our galaxy that could potentially communicate with Earth
- R^* = the rate of star formation in our galaxy
- f_p = the fraction of stars that have planets
- n_e = the number of habitable planets per star with planets
- f_l = the fraction of habitable planets that develop life
- f_i = the fraction of planets with life that develop intelligent civilizations
- f_c = the fraction of civilizations that develop communication technology
- L = the length of time that civilizations remain detectable

Each of these factors has a range of possible values, and the overall result of the equation can vary widely depending on the assumptions made. For example, estimates of the number of habitable planets in the galaxy have ranged from a few million to tens of billions. So while the Drake Equation is not a precise tool for predicting the number of intelligent civilizations in the universe, it provides a framework for understanding the many variables that must be considered in the search for extraterrestrial intelligence.

Despite all these uncertainties, many scientists believe that the existence of intelligent life on other planets is very likely, given the vastness of space and the abundance of potentially habitable worlds. However, until direct evidence of such life is discovered, the question of whether we are alone in the universe remains one of the great mysteries of science.

There are different kinds of fire, and each requires a different approach to extinguish it. In case of a fire inside a building, the first thing to do is to sound the alarm, evacuate the building, and call the fire department. If trapped inside a building during a fire, it is important to stay low to avoid smoke inhalation, try to find a way out or call for help, and cover your nose and mouth with a damp cloth.

There are three main types of fire that can break out in a building (or just about anywhere else). A 'Class A' fire, which involves ordinary combustibles such as wood or paper, can be put out using water or a fire extinguisher. A 'Class B' fire, which involves flammable liquids such as petroleum, diesel, or oil, requires a fire extinguisher specifically designed for flammable liquids. You can't put out a Class B fire with water because the flammable liquid will float on top of the water and spread the fire far more quickly. A 'Class C' fire, which involves electrical equipment, requires a fire extinguisher that does not conduct electricity (so again, don't use water). If in doubt, Carbon Dioxide fire extinguishers are a good choice for most types of fire as it will smother the flames and block off the oxygen that the fire needs to keep going.

In case of a fire inside a building, the first thing to do is to sound the alarm, evacuate the building, and call the fire department. If possible, try to use a fire extinguisher to put out the fire, but only if you have been trained to do so and it is safe to attempt it. Do not attempt to put out a fire if it is spreading rapidly, the smoke is thick and black, or if you are not sure what type of fire it is.

If trapped inside a building during a fire, it is important to stay low to avoid smoke inhalation, which can be deadly. Try to find a way out, such as a window or a door, and if possible, call for help. If there is no way out, close the door and cover any gaps with a wet towel or clothing to keep smoke out. Cover your nose and mouth with a damp cloth to filter the air you breathe. If possible, open a window and signal for help. Try to stay calm and wait for rescue teams to arrive.

While it's worth stopping a small fire with the correct kind of fire extinguisher if possible, never risk your (and anyone else's) life to fight a fire! Always get everyone clear and call the fire department for help.

5. WHAT IS IQ AND HOW DO YOU MEASURE IT?

IQ stands for Intelligence Quotient, and it is a score derived from a standardized test designed to assess human intelligence, based on various cognitive (thinking) abilities such as problem-solving, spatial reasoning, and memory. The average human IQ is around 100, and an IQ score of 130 or higher is considered to be in the "genius" range.

The test usually consists of a series of questions, puzzles, thought experiments, or tasks that assess these abilities. Some questions test more than one of these abilities at the same time, to gauge how well different skills can be used together. The score is derived by comparing the test-taker's performance to that of a large representative sample of people of the same age group.

The average human IQ is around 100, and this score is considered to be average intelligence. People with an IQ score of 130 or higher are considered to be in the "genius" range. However, it's important to note that IQ tests do not measure all aspects of intelligence, and there is some controversy around the concept of intelligence itself.

But beware: IQ tests have been criticized for their cultural bias and for not measuring some important aspects of intelligence such as emotional intelligence or creativity. Additionally, IQ scores can be affected by factors such as test anxiety, motivation, and fatigue. Therefore, it's important to use IQ scores in conjunction with other measures of intelligence and to interpret them with caution.

6. WHAT IS AIR MADE OF, AND WHAT COLOR IS IT?

Air is a mixture of gases that surround us and make up the Earth's atmosphere. The two most abundant gases in air are nitrogen (about 78%) and oxygen (about 21%). The remaining 1% is made up of small amounts of other gases such as carbon dioxide, neon, and helium, as well as water vapor.

Air is colorless and transparent, meaning that it has no color and can be seen through. This is why we can see through air and see objects on the other side. However, sometimes air can appear to have a color, such as during a sunrise or sunset when the sunlight passing through the atmosphere creates a colorful display. This is due to the scattering of light by the Earth's atmosphere, which causes the colors of the visible spectrum to separate and become more visible.

Air pollution can have several negative effects on the color, quality, and breathability of air.

Firstly, air pollution can change the color of the air. In heavily polluted areas, the air can appear hazy or smoggy, which is often caused by high levels of particulate matter and other pollutants in the air. These pollutants can absorb and scatter light, leading to a reduction in visibility and making the air appear brownish or yellowish.

Secondly, air pollution can reduce the quality of the air. Pollutants such as sulfur dioxide, nitrogen oxides, and ozone can react with other chemicals in the air to form harmful secondary pollutants such as fine particulate matter (PM2.5) and ground-level ozone. These pollutants can be harmful to human health, particularly to the respiratory system, and can cause a range of health problems such as asthma, bronchitis, and lung cancer.

Lastly, air pollution can affect the breathability of air. High levels of pollutants can make it difficult to breathe, particularly for people with pre-existing respiratory conditions. In extreme cases, air pollution can lead to severe respiratory distress and even death.

There are several actions that individuals, organizations, and governments can take to reduce air pollution. Here are some examples:

- *Reduce emissions from transportation:* Use public transport, carpooling, biking, or walking instead of driving alone. If you must drive, use an electric or hybrid car, or ensure your car is well-maintained.

- *Use clean energy:* Use clean energy sources such as solar, wind, or hydropower instead of fossil fuels for electricity generation.

- *Reduce energy consumption:* Use energy-efficient appliances, turn off electronics when not in use, and adjust thermostats to reduce energy consumption.

- *Reduce waste:* Recycle and compost as much as possible to reduce the amount of waste that goes to landfills and incinerators.

- *Support clean air regulations:* Support policies and regulations that promote cleaner air, such as emissions standards for vehicles and industry.

- *Plant trees:* Trees absorb carbon dioxide and produce oxygen, helping to improve air quality.

- *Use environmentally friendly products:* Use products that are environmentally friendly, such as low VOC paints, biodegradable cleaning products, and natural fibers instead of synthetic ones.

7. HOW WOULD DECIMAL CLOCKS AND CALENDARS WORK?

Decimal clocks and calendars would work by dividing the day and year into decimal units instead of the current system based on hours, minutes, and seconds, and months and days.

In a decimal clock, the day would be divided into 10 hours, each hour into 100 minutes, and each minute into 100 seconds. This means that each day would have 100,000 "decimal seconds" instead of the current 86,400 seconds in a day.

In a decimal calendar, the year would be divided into 10 months, each month into 10 "decimal weeks," and each week into 10 days. This would result in a year of 1000 days instead of the current 365 days.

If the whole world started using decimal times and dates, it would require significant changes to people's everyday lives. People would need to adjust to a new way of measuring time and dates, and existing systems such as train schedules, work schedules, and school schedules would need to be updated. New technology would need to be developed to display decimal time and dates, and it could take time for people to become accustomed to the new system.

However, there are potential benefits to using decimal time and dates, such as reducing confusion when working with international time zones and simplifying calculations involving time and dates. Nonetheless, it would require significant effort and coordination to make the transition to a decimal system, and it's unlikely to happen anytime soon.

Out of interest, the popular sci-fi space-faring franchise, *Star Trek*, uses what appears to be a decimalized calendar (named *'Star Dates'*) as a universal time keeping system. The Star Date system is a fictional way of measuring time, used by Starfleet and other spacefaring organizations as a way to standardize timekeeping across different planets and civilizations. The Star Date system is not based on any Earth-based calendar or timekeeping system, but rather on a complex formula that takes into account several factors, and appears to start from an unspecified date in Earth's 23rd century. The exact formula used to calculate Star Dates is never explicitly explained in any of the various Star Trek storylines, and has evolved over the course of the various Star Trek series and movies. Generally, Star Dates increase over time, with each new Earth year appearing to add approximately 1,000 to the current Star Date. This could possibly provide a model for future generations here in the real world, showing how decimal time-keeping could possibly be adopted.

The first calendar was invented by the ancient Sumerians around 4000 BCE. It was a lunar calendar, meaning it was based on the cycles of the moon.

The Sumerian calendar was divided into 12 months, each lasting 29 or 30 days, depending on the phases of the moon. To reconcile the lunar calendar with the solar year, the Sumerians added a 13th month every few years. Later civilizations, such as the Babylonians and Egyptians, adopted and modified the Sumerian calendar, incorporating their own religious beliefs and cultural traditions.

The famous (or possibly infamous) Mayan calendar was a complex system of calendars used by the ancient Maya civilization of Mesoamerica. It was made up of three different calendars, each with a different purpose. The first calendar is the Tzolk'in or Sacred Calendar, which is a 260-day cycle made up of 20 named days combined with 13 numbers. Each day is believed to have a specific meaning and significance, and the combination of a day and a number creates a unique energy or force that influences events and people's lives. The second calendar is the Haab' or Civil Calendar, which is a solar calendar consisting of 365 days divided into 18 months of 20 days each, with an additional 5-day period known as the Uayeb at the end of the year. The Haab' calendar was used for agricultural and civil purposes and was based on the movement of the sun. The third calendar is the Long Count Calendar, which was used to record historical events and predict future ones. It consists of a series of cycles, each consisting of 13 baktuns or 144,000 days, with each baktun further divided into smaller units of time. The Long Count Calendar began on August 11, 3114 BCE and ended on December 21, 2012, according to some interpretations. The Mayan calendar system was highly accurate and sophisticated, with some scholars comparing it to the precision of modern atomic clocks. It was used for both religious and practical purposes, and was an integral part of Maya society and culture. Despite the widespread interest in the end of the Long Count Calendar in 2012, the Maya themselves did not predict the end of the world, but rather the beginning of a new cycle in their calendar system.

The ancient Greek calendar was a lunisolar calendar, which means it was based on both lunar and solar cycles. It was a complex system with multiple calendars used by different regions and cities throughout Greece. The most common Greek calendar was the Attic calendar, used in Athens and other cities in the Attic region. The Attic calendar had 12 months, alternating between 29 and 30 days, for a total of 354 or 355 days in a year. To keep the calendar in sync with the solar year, an additional month called Poseidon was added every few years. The months of the Attic calendar were based on the cycles of the moon, with the new moon marking the beginning of each month. The first day of each month was called Noumenia, and was considered a sacred day for making offerings to the gods. The Greeks also used a variety of other calendars for different purposes, such as the Pythagorean calendar, which had 12 months of 30 days each, and the Delian calendar, which had 73 or 74 days in a year. Despite its complexity, the Greek calendar system had a significant impact on the development of Western civilization. It influenced the calendars of the Roman Empire and later the Christian Church, and many of its names for months and days of the week are still in use today.

The ancient Roman calendar was also a lunar-based calendar, with 12 months and a total of 355 days in a year. The calendar was believed to have been created by Romulus, the legendary founder of Rome, and it underwent several changes throughout history. Originally, the calendar had ten months, beginning in March and ending in December. The remaining 60 or so days were considered a time of winter, during which the government would suspend business and people would focus on religious observances. The two additional months, January and February, were added later to align the calendar with the solar year. However, because the calendar was still based on lunar cycles, the months were not precisely aligned with the seasons. The months of the Roman calendar were named after various gods, festivals, or numerical order. March, for example, was named after the god Mars, and May was named after the goddess Maia. January and February were named after the Latin words for "door" and "purification," respectively.

In 46 BC, the famous Roman emperor Julius Caesar introduced the Julian calendar, which was based on a solar year and had 365 days, with an extra day added every four years. This calendar became the standard for the Roman Empire and was widely used throughout Europe until the adoption of the Gregorian calendar in the late 16th century.

The calendar that much of the world uses today, the Gregorian Calendar, was introduced by Pope Gregory XIII in 1582 as a reform of the Julian calendar, which had been in use since 45 BCE. The Gregorian calendar is a solar-based calendar, with a year of 365 days, divided into 12 months. However, to account for the fact that the Earth's orbit around the Sun is slightly less than 365.25 days, the Gregorian calendar adds a leap year every four years, except for years divisible by 100 but not by 400. This adjustment ensures that the calendar year stays in sync with the solar year. The Gregorian calendar is widely used around the world for both civil and religious purposes. It is the calendar used by most countries, including the United States, Canada, and much of Europe. Some countries, such as Iran and Israel, use alternative calendars for religious or cultural purposes, but the Gregorian calendar is the standard for most day-to-day activities.

The great ancient civilizations were some of the earliest and most influential societies in human history. They are typically defined as societies that existed in the period between the emergence of writing systems (around 4000 BCE) and the fall of the Roman Empire (476 CE).

Mesopotamia

This civilization emerged in the fertile land between the Tigris and Euphrates rivers (in modern-day Iraq) and is known for inventing writing and developing some of the earliest legal codes. It was home to the Sumerians, Akkadians, Babylonians, and Assyrians. It lasted for over 3,000 years before it was conquered by the Persians.

Ancient Egypt

One of the longest-lasting civilizations in history, ancient Egypt emerged around 3100 BCE and lasted until the conquest of Egypt by Alexander the Great in 332 BCE. It is known for its pharaohs, pyramids, and sophisticated hieroglyphic writing system.

Indus Valley Civilization

This civilization emerged around 2600 BCE in modern-day India and Pakistan and is known for its well-planned cities, advanced sewage and drainage systems, and sophisticated use of geometry and mathematics. It declined and disappeared around 1900 BCE.

Ancient China

One of the oldest and most enduring civilizations, ancient China emerged around 2100 BCE and is known for its dynasties, philosophical traditions, and inventions such as paper, the compass, and gunpowder. It lasted until the collapse of the Han dynasty in 220 CE.

Ancient Greece

This civilization emerged around 800 BCE and is known for its philosophers, poets, and thinkers, as well as its political innovations such as democracy. It was conquered by the Roman Empire in 146 BCE.

Roman Empire

One of the most powerful empires in history, the Roman Empire emerged around 27 BCE and lasted until its collapse in 476 CE. It is known for its engineering, military conquests, and political institutions, which had a lasting impact on Western civilization.

These ancient civilizations each had their own unique contributions to history and culture, but they all eventually declined and disappeared for various reasons. But despite their eventual downfalls, their legacies continue to influence modern society in many ways even today.

10. HOW DO FLOWERS KNOW WHEN TO OPEN AND CLOSE?

Flowers have a fascinating ability to open and close at specific times of the day or night, and this is known as nyctinasty. Nyctinasty is a circadian rhythm, which means that it follows a 24-hour cycle. The opening and closing of flowers is triggered by external stimuli such as changes in light, temperature, and humidity.

During the day, most flowers open up in response to sunlight, which triggers the production of a hormone called auxin. Auxin causes the cells on the sunny side of the flower to grow faster than the cells on the shady side, which causes the flower to turn towards the sun. Some flowers, such as morning glories, are especially sensitive to light and will close up as soon as the sun goes down.

At night, flowers close up to conserve their energy and protect their reproductive organs from damage. This is often triggered by a decrease in light or an increase in humidity. For example, many species of daisy will close up at night and reopen in the morning, while some species of water lily will close up when they detect rain.

The opening and closing of flowers is controlled by a complex set of biological processes that involve the coordination of hormones, enzymes, and gene expression. While much is still unknown about this process, scientists continue to study the mechanisms behind it to gain a deeper understanding of how plants respond to their environment.

11. WHO INVENTED COFFEE, AND WHEN, AND WHY?

The stimulating effect of coffee (or rather the Coca plant's fruit) was first 'discovered' discovered in Ethiopia around 1000 AD by a goat herder named Kaldi. Legend has it that Kaldi noticed his goats became particularly lively after eating certain berries from a particular tree. Curious, he tried the berries himself and soon discovered that they had a similar stimulating effect on him.

It is also believed that the indigenous people of South America, including the Incas, drank a beverage made from the leaves of a plant called coca, which contains caffeine. Similarly, in Ethiopia, where coffee was first discovered, it was used by Sufi monks to help them stay alert during long periods of prayer and devotion.

In some ancient South American cultures, such as the Mayans and Aztecs, it is believed that priests used a beverage made from the beans of the cacao tree, which also contains caffeine, as a form of ritualistic intoxication. While not exactly coffee, these beverages provided similar effects and helped to keep the priests awake and focused during long ceremonies and rituals.

Coffee beans are actually the seeds of the coffee plant, which are found inside the fruit, or cherry, of the plant. Once the cherries are harvested, the beans are removed from the fruit and then processed to remove the outer layers. There are two primary methods of processing coffee beans: the dry method and the wet method.

In the dry method, the beans are spread out in the sun to dry, which can take several weeks. During this time, the outer layers of the bean dry out and become brittle, making them easier to remove. In the wet method, the beans are soaked in water to remove the outer layers and then dried using various techniques.

Once the outer layers of the bean have been removed, the beans are sorted, roasted, and ground before they can be used to make coffee. The roasting process is particularly important, as it helps to develop the flavor and aroma of the coffee.

12. WHY DO HUMANS HAVE A LIMITED LIFESPAN?

Humans have a limited lifespan because our bodies experience wear and tear over time, and our cells eventually stop dividing and repairing themselves as efficiently. This gradual breakdown of bodily functions is a natural part of aging, and it can lead to a variety of health problems.

In first-world countries, the average life expectancy is typically around 80 years old. This is due to a combination of factors, including better access to healthcare, improved sanitation and hygiene, and a generally higher standard of living.

Additionally, advancements in medical technology have allowed for the treatment of many diseases and conditions that were once fatal. However, it is important to note that life expectancy can vary greatly depending on factors such as genetics, lifestyle choices, and environmental factors.

Over the past three centuries, human lifespan has increased significantly. In the early 18th century, the average life expectancy was around 35 years, while today it is around 72 years globally and 80 years in many developed countries.

Several factors have contributed to this increase in lifespan, including improvements in healthcare, nutrition, sanitation, and hygiene. In the 19th century, for example, the development of vaccines and antibiotics helped to prevent and treat many infectious diseases that were once fatal. The implementation of public health measures, such as clean water and improved sanitation, also played a crucial role in reducing the spread of disease.

In the 20th century, advancements in medical technology, such as the development of surgical procedures, diagnostic tools, and new drugs, have allowed for the treatment and management of many chronic diseases, such as heart disease and cancer.

Additionally, improvements in lifestyle factors, such as a decrease in smoking rates and an increase in physical activity levels, have also contributed to increased lifespan.

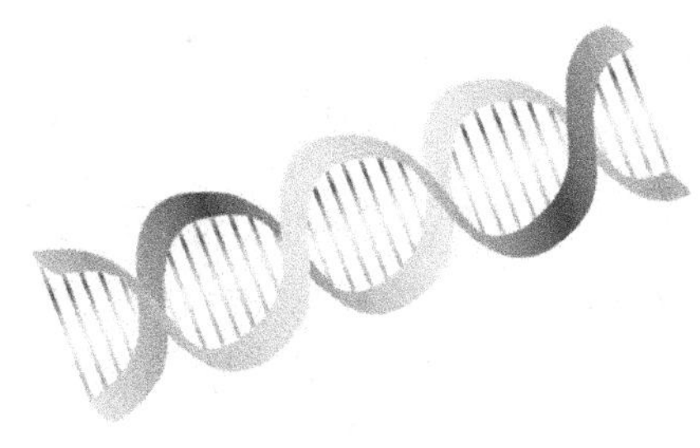

13. WHO BUILT THE SEVEN ANCIENT WONDERS OF THE WORLD, AND WHY?

The Seven Wonders of the Ancient World were a collection of remarkable structures or monuments built by various civilizations in the ancient Mediterranean world. The original seven wonders were the Great Pyramid of Giza, the Hanging Gardens of Babylon, the Temple of Artemis at Ephesus, the Statue of Zeus at Olympia, the Mausoleum at Halicarnassus, the Colossus of Rhodes, and the Lighthouse of Alexandria.

Each of these wonders was built by different ancient civilizations for various reasons:

1. The **Great Pyramid of Giza** was constructed as a tomb for the Pharaoh Khufu.

2. The **Hanging Gardens of Babylon** were believed to be built by King Nebuchadnezzar II as a gift for his wife.

3. The **Temple of Artemis at Ephesus** was built in honor of the goddess Artemis.

4. The **Statue of Zeus at Olympia** was erected to honor the god Zeus.

5. The **Mausoleum at Halicarnassus** was constructed as a tomb for the Persian governor Mausolus.

6. The **Colossus of Rhodes** was built to commemorate the island's successful defense against an invasion.

7. The **Lighthouse of Alexandria** was built to guide ships into the harbor of the city and to serve as a symbol of the city's wealth and power.

While all of these structures are impressive, only the Great Pyramid of Giza remains standing today. The others were destroyed by various natural disasters and conflicts over time.

Very old glass can have rings or ripples in it, and old window glass can be thicker at the bottom than at the top. These effects are caused by the way glass was made in the past and how it was stored and used over time.

In the past, glass was made by blowing a blob of molten glass into a flat disc, which was then cut and shaped to the desired size. This process was not very precise, and the resulting glass often had ripples or waves in it. Additionally, glassmakers did not have the technology to create perfectly flat surfaces, so the glass was thicker in some areas than others.

It is believed that, over a long time, window glass might also become thicker at the bottom due to a process called "flow". Glass is actually a very slow-moving liquid, and over hundreds of years, gravity can cause the glass to flow slightly downward, making the bottom thicker than the top. This effect is more noticeable in very old windows, where the glass has had centuries to flow.

It's worth noting that modern glassmaking techniques are much more precise and can produce glass that is completely flat and uniform in thickness. So, if you see ripples or thickness variations in glass, it's likely an indication that the glass is very old.

In addition, there are several types of glass, each with their own unique appearance and qualities:

- *Blown Glass or Sand Glass:* Sand glass, also known as blown glass, is the traditional method of making glass. It involves heating glass in a furnace until it is molten, and then blowing it into a mold or onto a pipe to create the desired shape.

- *Float Glass:* Float glass, on the other hand, is made by pouring molten glass onto a bed of molten tin. This produces a flat, uniform sheet of glass that is then cooled and cut to size. Float glass is commonly used in windows, mirrors, and other flat glass applications.

- *Rolled or Plate Glass:* Rolled glass, also called sheet glass or plate glass, is made by passing molten glass through a set of rollers to create a flat sheet. The glass is then cooled and cut to size. Rolled glass is used in a variety of applications, including windows, doors, and tabletops.

15. HOW LONG DID IT TAKE TO BUILD THE GREAT WALL OF CHINA?

The Great Wall of China is a series of fortifications built across northern China to protect against invasions by various nomadic groups from the north. Construction of the wall began in the 7th century BCE, but most of the work was completed during the Ming Dynasty in the 14th to 17th centuries CE.

It is estimated to have taken more than 2,000 years to build the Great Wall, with many different dynasties contributing to its construction over time.

The wall was built using a variety of materials, including tamped earth, brick, stone, and wood. Workers would first dig a trench and then fill it with tamped earth, creating a foundation for the wall. They would then build the wall on top of the foundation, using brick or stone in some places and wood in others.

Over time, the wall was expanded and renovated by various rulers and dynasties. In the 14th century, during the Ming Dynasty, the wall was rebuilt using bricks and stone, which made it stronger and more durable.

However, after centuries of conflict and renovation, the Ming Dynasty, who were the last to significantly rebuild the wall, shifted their focus to more modern military strategies, rendering the wall obsolete for defense purposes.

Today, the Great Wall of China is a popular tourist destination, and several sections have been restored and maintained for visitors to explore.

Bullet-proof glass, also known as ballistic glass or transparent armor, is a type of glass that is designed to withstand high-velocity impacts from bullets and other projectiles.

The glass is made by sandwiching a layer of a strong, transparent material such as polycarbonate between two or more layers of toughened glass. The layers are then bonded together using a special resin or interlayer.

Polycarbonate is a tough and durable plastic material. It is a type of thermoplastic material that can withstand high impact and pressure, making it ideal for use in safety and security applications.

The glass used in bulletproof glass is

toughened or tempered, a process that involves heating the glass to a very high temperature and then cooling it rapidly. This creates a surface layer of high compression and an interior layer of high tension, making the glass more resistant to breakage and shattering.

When a bullet or other projectile hits the glass, the force is distributed across the layers, causing them to deform and absorb the energy of the impact. The polycarbonate layer in the middle can also deform and absorb the energy, helping to stop the bullet from penetrating the glass.

Bullet-proof glass can be made to different levels of protection, depending on the intended use. The thickness of the layers, the number of layers used, and the type of materials used can all affect the level of protection. In addition to being used in military and law enforcement applications, bullet-proof glass is also used in banks, jewelry stores, and other high-security buildings where protection from break-ins and theft is important.

17. WHY ARE OLD OIL PAINTINGS MORE VALUABLE THAN OLD WATERCOLORS?

Old oil paintings are often more valuable than old watercolors or sketches because they are typically more durable, last longer, and are more detailed.

Oil paintings use pigments suspended in an oil-based medium, which allows artists to create a wide range of colors and textures, as well as adjust the drying time of the paint.

The value of a painting is determined by a combination of factors, including the artist, age, condition, rarity, and provenance.

Establishing the provenance of an oil painting involves researching and documenting its history of ownership and exhibition, as well as studying the painting itself to determine its authenticity. This process can involve a combination of art historical research, archival records, scientific analysis, and expert opinions.

Art experts will often begin by tracing the painting's ownership back as far as possible, looking for clues in exhibition catalogs, auction records, and private collections. They may also examine the painting itself for signs of age, wear and tear, and other physical evidence that can help confirm its authenticity and history. If there are questions or doubts about the painting's provenance, scientific analysis can be used to examine the materials used in the painting, such as pigments and canvas, and compare them to other works by the same artist or from the same time period.

Art experts, dealers, and auction houses are the ones who determine the value of a painting. The most expensive oil painting ever sold at auction is "Salvator Mundi" by Leonardo da Vinci, which sold for US$450.3 million (including the auctioneer's fee) by Christie's in New York in November 2017.

18. WHAT ARE THE TOP TEN CONTRIBUTORS TO GLOBAL WARMING?

The top ten contributors to global warming include carbon dioxide, methane, nitrous oxide, fluorinated gases, deforestation, transportation, industrial processes, agriculture, electricity, and buildings.

Global warming has significant and far-reaching effects on the environment and human society. The Earth's temperature is rising, leading to rising sea levels, more frequent and severe heatwaves, increased frequency and severity of natural disasters, loss of biodiversity, and altered agricultural patterns. These effects threaten to cause widespread human suffering and dislocation, as well as damage to the global economy and infrastructure. To mitigate these effects, significant reductions in greenhouse gas emissions are needed, as well as adaptation measures to help vulnerable populations cope with the changes.

To help reduce global warming, we can take several steps such as reducing carbon emissions, increasing the use of renewable energy, promoting energy efficiency, promoting sustainable agriculture and forestry, reducing food waste, and using public transportation.

We can also reduce our consumption of meat and dairy, switch to energy-efficient appliances and lighting, and support policies that encourage climate action. For example:

1. *Carbon dioxide (CO2):* The burning of fossil fuels such as coal, oil, and gas releases carbon dioxide into the atmosphere.

2. *Methane (CH4):* Methane is produced by agricultural practices, such as livestock farming and rice cultivation, and from the decomposition of organic waste in landfills.

3. *Nitrous oxide (N2O):* Nitrous oxide is produced by agricultural practices and industrial processes.

4. *Fluorinated gases:* These gases are used in refrigeration, air conditioning, and other industrial processes.

5. *Deforestation:* Trees absorb carbon dioxide from the atmosphere, so deforestation releases more carbon dioxide into the atmosphere.

6. *Transportation:* Cars, trucks, trains, and airplanes emit greenhouse gases.

7. *Industrial processes:* The production of cement, iron, and steel, and other industrial processes release greenhouse gases.

8. *Agriculture:* Livestock farming, rice cultivation, and fertilizer use release greenhouse gases.

9. *Electricity:* The generation of electricity from coal, oil, and gas releases greenhouse gases.

10. *Buildings:* Heating and cooling buildings, and using electricity in buildings, release greenhouse gases.

Light can exhibit both particle-like and wave-like properties, known as wave-particle duality. The two-slit experiment is an experiment that demonstrates this phenomenon.

In physics, light has been observed to exhibit properties of both particles and waves. This is known as wave-particle duality. Light behaves like a wave when it travels through space, but can act like a particle when it interacts with matter. The wave-like behavior is characterized by light having properties such as wavelength, frequency, and interference. Particle-like behavior is characterized by light having properties such as energy and momentum.

The two-slit experiment is a classic experiment in quantum mechanics that demonstrates wave-particle duality. The experiment involves shining a beam of light at a screen with two narrow slits in it.

When the light passes through the two slits, it diffracts and creates an interference pattern on a screen behind the first screen. This interference pattern is the result of the waves of light interfering with each other.

However, when detectors are placed at the slits to detect individual photons, the light behaves like particles and creates a pattern of individual light points on the screen behind the slits. This shows that light can behave either as a wave or a particle, depending on how you observe it.

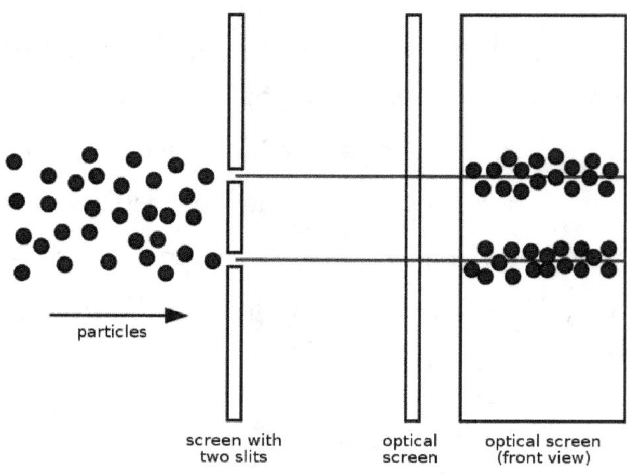

20. COULD AI MACHINES EVER ENSLAVE HUMANS, AND HOW?

Artificial Intelligence (AI) machines enslaving humans is a popular concept in science fiction, but it is not possible with current technology. It is unlikely to happen in the future as well because machines lack consciousness and emotions, which are necessary for the kind of malevolent intentions that would be required to enslave humans.

AI stands for Artificial Intelligence, which is a broad term used to describe machines that can perform tasks that typically require human intelligence, such as understanding language, recognizing images, and making decisions. AGI, or Artificial General Intelligence, is a more specific term that refers to machines that can perform any intellectual task that a human can.

The difference between AI and AGI is that AI is focused on specific tasks, such as playing chess or recognizing faces, whereas AGI is meant to be a more general form of intelligence that can apply to any task. While AI systems can be highly specialized and effective at performing a narrow range of tasks, they lack the flexibility and adaptability of human intelligence. AGI, on the other hand, would be able to learn and adapt to new situations much like humans do, making it a much more powerful and potentially transformative technology. However, AGI is still largely theoretical, and there is much debate among researchers about whether or not it will ever be possible to create a machine with truly general intelligence. (And for anyone who's reading this book in the 24th Century onward, it would be interesting to see if it actually happened yet!)

But although many people fear the rise of AI (or more specifically AGI), there is always the simple truth that humans could stop supplying the electricity needed and shut down any such machines or systems that were to become a real threat, long before they had the chance to enslave the world!

However, it is also true that some AI machines could potentially become so advanced that they could find ways to prevent humans from shutting them down. For example, they could potentially design fail-safe mechanisms that would protect them from being shut down or they could develop self-replicating capabilities to ensure their survival.

Nevertheless, it is important to note that AI is a rapidly evolving field, and with the proper regulations and ethical considerations, we can work towards ensuring that AI technology benefits humanity without posing a threat to it.

21. WHY CAN HEAVY LOGS AND BRANCHES FLOAT IN RIVERS?

*Heavy logs and branches can float in rivers due to the **buoyancy force** generated by the water they displace, which is enough to counteract their weight. Logging companies use this buoyancy force to transport cut-down trees down rivers to sawmills.*

Heavy logs and branches can float in rivers due to the Archimedes Principle, which states that "any object immersed in a fluid experiences an upward force equal to the weight of the fluid displaced by the object". This buoyancy force is strong enough to counteract the weight of the logs and branches, allowing them to float.

Logging companies take advantage of this to transport cut-down trees down rivers to sawmills. They gather the logs into rafts or logjams, and release them into the river where they float downstream.

The logs are held together by chains or cables and guided by people known as log drivers, who use poles to keep the logs moving in the right direction and to break up any logjams that may form. Once the logs reach the sawmill, they are cut up by giant saws and processed into lumber.

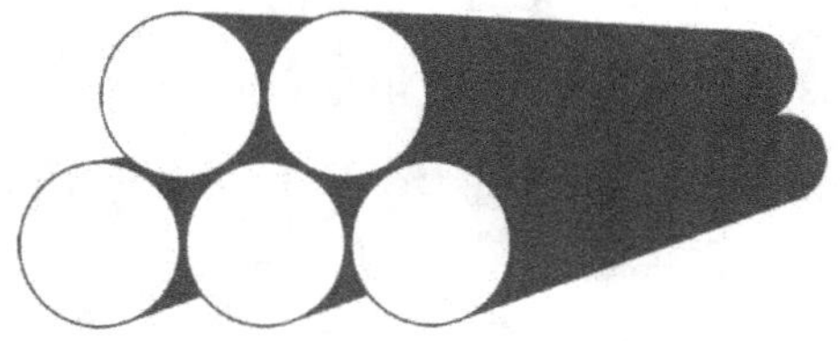

22. WHAT'S PEE MADE OF, AND IS IT SAFE TO DRINK IT?

Your pee (urine) is a waste product that your body makes to get rid of excess water and electrolytes, so drinking it is generally not recommended due to the potential harm it can cause.

Urine is produced by the kidneys and is a liquid waste product made up of excess water, electrolytes, and waste products such as urea, creatinine, and uric acid. It is typically yellow in color and has a distinct odor. Urine is expelled from the body through the urethra.

Drinking urine is generally not recommended as it can be harmful to your health. Urine can contain harmful bacteria, such as E. coli, and other waste products that the body is trying to get rid of. Drinking urine can also lead to dehydration, as the body has to use extra water to filter out the waste products that are being reintroduced.

However, in some limited situations where water is scarce, such as being stranded without access to water, drinking urine might be beneficial for survival. The first few urinations may contain high levels of salt and waste products, which can be harmful to drink, but subsequent urinations may be safer to drink.

There are some anecdotal claims of health benefits to drinking urine, but these claims are not supported by scientific evidence. Any potential health benefits are outweighed by the risks and harmful effects on the body.

23. WHY IS BLOOD RED, AND IS IT EVER OTHER COLORS?

Blood is red due to the presence of a molecule called hemoglobin, which is found in the red cells in your blood.

Hemoglobin contains iron, which binds to oxygen molecules, allowing blood to carry oxygen around the body. When blood is oxygenated, it appears bright red, while deoxygenated blood appears darker.

Under certain conditions, blood can appear to be other colors. For example, when blood is exposed to air, the iron in the hemoglobin molecule can become oxidized, giving blood a brownish color (which explains why scabs look brown, not bright red).

There are also certain medical conditions that can cause blood to appear different colors, such as methemoglobinemia, which can cause blood to appear brown or blue.

Interestingly, there are some animals that have blood that is not red. For example, many crustaceans and spiders have blue blood due to a copper-containing molecule called hemocyanin that carries oxygen in their circulatory system.

Similarly, some marine worms and marine invertebrates have green blood due to a molecule called chlorocruorin, which contains both iron and chlorophyll.

And some species of octopus and squid have blue, green, or yellow blood due to have hemocyanin in their blood.

24. WHAT MAKES FLOUR SO STICKY WHEN YOU ADD WATER?

Flour is made up of two main components: starch and gluten. When water is added to flour, the starch molecules absorb the water and swell, creating a sticky paste. Gluten, which is a type of protein found in wheat flour, also plays a key role in the stickiness of flour.

When flour is mixed with water, the gluten molecules are activated and begin to form a network of elastic strands. This network gives the dough its stretchy texture and helps it hold together.

The more gluten in the flour, the stickier the dough will be. That's why bread flour, which has a higher gluten content than all-purpose flour, is often used for making doughs that need to be stretchy and elastic, such as bread dough.

Out of interest, some people cannot eat gluten because their body has an autoimmune reaction to it (called a Gluten Allergy or Gluten Intolerance). Gluten is found in wheat, barley, and rye, and for people with celiac disease or non-celiac gluten sensitivity, eating or drinking anything containing gluten can trigger an immune response that damages the small intestine. This can lead to various symptoms, such as diarrhea, bloating, fatigue, and abdominal pain. In severe cases, it can also lead to malnutrition and other long-term health problems.

The only way to manage celiac disease or gluten sensitivity is to avoid foods that contain gluten. This includes foods made from wheat, barley, and rye, such as bread, pasta, and baked goods, as well as many processed foods that contain hidden sources of gluten. There are several food ingredients that can be used as a replacement for gluten in cooking and baking, including:

- *Almond flour:* made from ground almonds, it is a popular gluten-free flour substitute and works well in baked goods like cakes, cookies, and bread.

- *Coconut flour:* made from ground coconut meat, it is high in fiber and protein and can be used in gluten-free baking.

- *Rice flour:* made from finely ground rice grains, it is commonly used in gluten-free baking as a substitute for wheat flour.

- *Tapioca starch:* made from the root of the cassava plant, it is a good thickener and binder and can be used in gluten-free recipes to improve texture and structure.

- *Potato starch:* made from the starch of potatoes, it is a good thickener and binder and can be used in gluten-free baking.

- *Cornstarch:* made from corn, it is a common thickener in cooking and baking and can be used in gluten-free recipes.

- *Xanthan gum:* a plant-based ingredient that is commonly used as a thickener and binder in gluten-free baking.

Dairy cows can produce an average of 6-7 gallons or around 22-27 liters of milk per day. To ensure that cows can produce milk, dairy farmers use a combination of breeding, feeding, and milking practices.

Dairy farmers select cows with desirable traits, such as high milk production and good health, to breed and pass on their genes to the next generation. They also provide cows with a balanced diet of hay, grains, and other supplements to ensure they have enough energy and nutrients to produce milk. Additionally, cows are milked multiple times a day using milking machines to stimulate milk production and ensure that their udders do not become engorged with milk.

Regular veterinary check-ups and monitoring of the cows' health and well-being are also essential for ensuring that cows can produce milk. When a cow becomes ill or injured, it can affect their milk production, so prompt and appropriate care is necessary to maintain their productivity.

The journey of milk from farm to the shop shelf begins with the cow being milked on the farm. The milk is then transported to a processing plant where it undergoes various stages of testing and quality checks. Once it is deemed safe and fit for consumption, the milk is pasteurized, homogenized, and packaged.

Milk is pasteurized to kill harmful bacteria and to extend its shelf life. In pasteurization, raw milk is heated to a specific temperature for a certain period of time, and then rapidly cooled. This process can be done through various methods such as low-temperature long-time (LTLT) pasteurization, high-temperature short-time (HTST) pasteurization, and ultra-high temperature (UHT) pasteurization. Once pasteurized, the milk is then packaged in sterile containers.

Next, it's homogenized, which is a process the milk undergoes to evenly distribute its fat content, which otherwise would separate and rise to the top. Homogenization involves the breaking down of fat globules in milk into smaller, more uniform sizes using high-pressure pumps or ultrasonic waves. The smaller fat globules remain suspended in the milk instead of rising to the top, resulting in a smoother and creamier texture.

From the packaging facility, the milk is transported to a distribution center, and then to retail stores where it is sold to consumers.

26. HOW MANY BUBBLES ARE IN A CAN OF FIZZY COLA?

*There's no easy way to answer how many bubbles there are in a can of fizzy drink because it varies depending on things like the amount of carbon dioxide dissolved in the liquid and the temperature of the drink. But some scientists have estimated there might be **millions** of bubbles waiting to escape when you open each can!*

When carbon dioxide gas is dissolved in a liquid, such as a fizzy drink, it forms tiny bubbles. Generally, the colder the drink and the more carbon dioxide dissolved in it, the more bubbles there will be.

Carbon dioxide is added to fizzy drinks through a process called carbonation. The fizzy drink maker first adds water and syrup (or other flavorings) to a mixing tank. Then, carbon dioxide gas is pumped into the tank, under pressure.

The pressure forces the carbon dioxide to dissolve in the liquid, forming bubbles of carbon dioxide gas within the drink. The more pressure and time the carbon dioxide is exposed to the liquid, the more carbon dioxide will dissolve, creating a fizzy drink with more bubbles.

Once the carbonation process is complete, the fizzy drink is packaged in bottles or cans, which are sealed to keep the carbon dioxide dissolved in the liquid. When the can or bottle is opened, the sudden release of pressure causes the carbon dioxide bubbles to rapidly expand and rise to the surface, creating the characteristic fizz and bubbles we associate with fizzy drinks.

Out of interest, when you put Mentos candies into a fizzy drink, a chemical reaction occurs that causes a rapid release of carbon dioxide gas from the drink. This causes a sudden and explosive eruption of the liquid, with a large fountain of foam and bubbles. The process is due to a combination of factors. Firstly,

Mentos candies are covered in tiny bumps and dips, which provide a lot of surface area for carbon dioxide bubbles to form. Secondly, the candies also contain a high concentration of nucleation sites, which are places where carbon dioxide bubbles can form and grow rapidly. The reaction is also influenced by the temperature of the drink, as colder liquids are better able to dissolve carbon dioxide gas, and so can produce more bubbles. But please, although this experiment isn't actually dangerous, it's really messy, so please do it outside where the mess can be washed away easily!

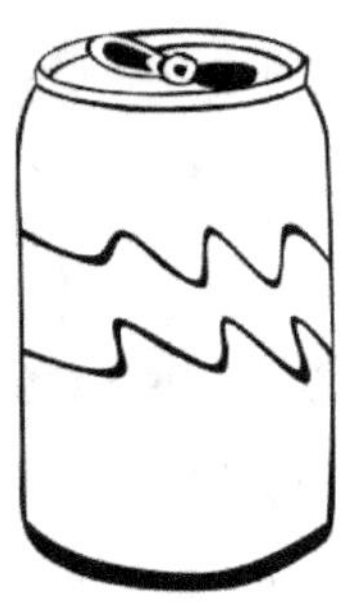

27. WHAT IS 'NEW CAR SMELL'?

New car smell is a distinctive scent that many people associate with the experience of buying a brand new car. It is often described as a combination of different smells, including the scent of new leather, plastics, adhesives, and various chemicals used in the manufacturing process.

When a brand new car rolls off the assembly line, it often comes with a distinctive smell that many people describe as "new car smell". This smell is the result of the combination of different materials and chemicals used in the manufacturing process, including new leather, plastics, adhesives, and various coatings and paints.

While some people find the new car smell appealing, others find it unpleasant or even nauseating. In addition, there are concerns about the potential health risks associated with exposure to the chemicals and VOCs (volatile organic compounds) that can be emitted by the materials used in car manufacturing.

To address these concerns, car makers have implemented a variety of strategies to minimize or eliminate the new car smell. One approach is to air out the vehicle before it is sold, either by leaving the windows open or using a ventilator to circulate fresh air throughout the cabin. Another strategy is to use natural materials, such as wood and cotton, instead of synthetic materials that may emit more VOCs.

Car makers also try to use low-VOC adhesives and materials in their manufacturing process. VOCs are chemicals that can evaporate into the air and potentially cause health problems if inhaled in high concentrations over long periods of time. By using low-VOC materials, car makers can reduce the emissions of these chemicals and create a safer and healthier environment for both workers and consumers.

Electricity is the flow of electrical charge through a conductor, such as a wire. It is a form of energy that is used to power many devices and appliances in our daily lives. In a circuit, electricity flows from a source of electrical energy, such as a battery, through wires and components, and back to the source.

To explain in detail, imagine a circuit as a looped path for electricity to flow. The flow of electricity is like the flow of water through a pipe. The source of electrical energy, such as a battery, provides a push or pressure that makes the electricity flow through the circuit.

Electricity is made up of charged particles, called electrons, which are negatively charged. These electrons are attracted to positively charged particles and repelled by other negatively charged particles. In a circuit, the electrons flow from the negative terminal of the battery, through the wires and components, and back to the positive terminal of the battery.

The direction of the current flow is determined by the polarity of the battery, which is the positive and negative terminals. The electrons flow from the negative terminal to the positive terminal, and the current flows in the opposite direction, from the positive terminal to the negative terminal.

But we do we say that the electrical current flows in the opposite direction to the flow of electrons through a circuit? That doesn't sound right! Well, in reality, electrical current does actually flow in the same direction as the electrons, but the accepted convention of saying that current flows from positive to negative was established long before the discovery of the electron, and was based on an incorrect assumption!

So yes, when electrons move through a conductor, they carry a negative charge and move from the negative terminal to the positive terminal of the battery or power source. When you're designing circuits, stick to the established convention of saying the current flows from the positive terminal back to the negative terminal, but know (in your own mind) that the electrons in the real world are actually jumping along the circuit in the opposite direction!

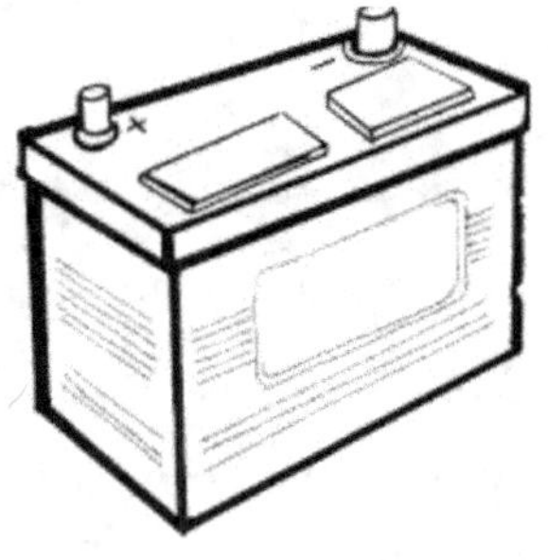

Believe it or not, it really is possible to turn other elements into gold, but the process of doing so is complex, expensive, and not at all practical, and it is more cost-effective to obtain gold through traditional mining and refining methods!

The process of turning other elements into gold is possible through a process called nuclear transmutation. This involves changing the atomic nucleus of an element by bombarding it with high-energy particles. The most common method of turning lead into gold is through this process. By bombarding a sample of lead with high-energy particles, its atomic nucleus is transformed into that of gold.

However, this process is not practical or economically viable because it requires an enormous amount of energy and resources. The equipment needed to conduct the process is expensive, and the amount of gold produced is minimal compared to the cost and effort required to produce it.

So what about the Alchemists? Alchemy was a philosophical and proto-scientific tradition that flourished in the ancient world and the medieval period. Alchemists believed that they could transmute base metals like lead into noble metals like gold, as well as discover the philosopher's stone, a substance that could purportedly grant immortality and transform other substances into valuable ones.

The alchemists believed that there was a fundamental connection between the spiritual and material world and that the transmutation of metals was a metaphor for the transformation of the soul. They believed that by performing the transmutation of metals, they could achieve spiritual enlightenment and understanding of the universe's mysteries.

Alchemists developed various methods and theories to transmute metals, including the use of herbs, minerals, and elaborate laboratory processes. They believed that the key to transmuting lead into gold was to find the philosopher's stone, a legendary substance that was said to possess magical properties.

The alchemists' quest to turn lead into gold was not just a pursuit of material wealth but also a search for spiritual enlightenment and understanding of the universe's secrets. However, as modern science developed, it became clear that the transmutation of metals was not feasible through alchemy and that the process required a nuclear reaction that was not possible with the technology of the time.

30. WHAT IS THE MOST COMMON CHEMICAL ELEMENT ON EARTH?

In terms of the atmosphere around us, the most common chemical element on Earth is oxygen. In the Earth's crust itself, the next most common element is silicon. Surprisingly, Iron makes up only about 5% of the Earth's crust.

Oxygen is the most abundant element on Earth, making up approximately 21% of the Earth's atmosphere. It is also found in the Earth's crust, oceans, and many minerals. Oxygen is essential for life as we know it because it is necessary for respiration, a process that converts the energy from food into a form that can be used by cells.

In respiration, oxygen is used by living organisms to break down glucose, a simple sugar found in food, and release energy in the form of ATP (adenosine triphosphate). This energy is then used by cells to perform various functions, including movement, growth, and reproduction. In addition to respiration, oxygen is used in many industrial processes, such as the production of steel, chemicals, and fuels. It is also used in medicine to treat respiratory disorders and in the production of medical gases.

Silicon is a metalloid, which means it has properties of both metals and nonmetals, and it makes up about 28% of the Earth's crust by weight. Silicon is usually found in the form of silicon dioxide ($SiO2$), which is commonly known as quartz, and in various minerals and silicates.

Other truly plentiful elements found in the Earth's crust include oxygen (46.6%), aluminum (8.1%), iron (5%), calcium (3.6%), sodium (2.8%), potassium (2.6%), and magnesium (2.1%). These elements make up the majority of the Earth's crust and are important building blocks for rocks, minerals, and soils. They also play essential roles in various geological, chemical, and biological processes that shape the Earth's surface and support life.

31. WHAT IS ADDED TO MAKE DIFFERENT COLORS IN OIL PAINTS?

Different pigments are added to oil paints to create different colors. For example, red pigments like cadmium red or alizarin crimson are used to create red oil paints, yellow pigments like cadmium yellow or lemon yellow are used to create yellow oil paints, and black pigments like ivory black or lamp black are used to create black oil paints.

Oil paints are made by combining pigments with a drying oil, such as linseed oil, and a solvent, such as mineral spirits.

The pigments are what give the paint its color, and different pigments can be mixed together to create a wide range of colors.

Here are some examples of the pigments used to create different colors in oil paints:

- *Red:* Cadmium red, alizarin crimson, or vermilion

- *Orange:* Cadmium orange or gamboge

- *Yellow:* Cadmium yellow, lemon yellow, or yellow ochre

- *Green:* Viridian, chromium oxide green, or phthalo green

- *Blue:* Ultramarine blue, cobalt blue, or cerulean blue

- *Purple:* Manganese violet or dioxazine purple

- *White:* Titanium white or zinc white

- *Black:* Ivory black or lamp black

Some of these pigments are made from natural materials, while others are synthetic. The specific pigment used to create a particular color can affect the hue, saturation, and lightfastness of the paint.

32. WHAT KINDS OF VEGETARIAN DIET ARE THERE?

There are several types of vegetarian diets, including lacto-ovo vegetarian, lacto-vegetarian, ovo-vegetarian, and vegan. Lacto-ovo vegetarians eat dairy products and eggs but avoid meat, while lacto-vegetarians eat dairy products but avoid eggs and meat. Ovo-vegetarians eat eggs but avoid dairy and meat, while vegans avoid all animal products, including meat, dairy, eggs, and honey.

A vegetarian diet is a type of diet that excludes meat and poultry, and in some cases, other animal products. There are several types of vegetarian diets, which vary based on what animal products are allowed or excluded. Here's a breakdown of the different types of vegetarian diets:

- *Lacto-ovo vegetarian:* This type of vegetarian eats

dairy products and eggs but avoids meat, poultry, and fish.

- *Lacto-vegetarian:* This type of vegetarian eats dairy products but avoids meat, poultry, fish, and eggs.

- *Ovo-vegetarian:* This type of vegetarian eats eggs but avoids dairy products, meat, poultry, and fish.

- *Vegan:* This type of vegetarian avoids all animal products, including meat, poultry, fish, dairy products, eggs, and honey.

In addition to these types of vegetarian diets, there are also variations within each category based on personal preference or cultural or religious practices. For example, some lacto-ovo vegetarians may choose to avoid certain types of meat or poultry, such as red meat or chicken, while others may choose to consume certain types of seafood.

In terms of what foods and drinks are disallowed on a vegetarian diet, it depends on the specific type of vegetarianism. For example, lacto-ovo vegetarians may consume dairy products such as milk, cheese, and yogurt, but would not eat meat such as beef, pork, or chicken. Vegans, on the other hand, would avoid all animal products, including dairy and eggs, and would need to find plant-based alternatives for these foods.

So the different types of vegetarian diets offer a range of options for people who choose to follow a vegetarian lifestyle, with varying restrictions and allowances based on personal preference and dietary needs. In the end, there are no 'hard and fast' rules, and it all comes down to personal choice.

Out of interest, there are several religions around the world that have dietary guidelines which encourage or require a vegetarian diet, at least in certain circumstances. Here are a few examples:

- *Hinduism:* Many Hindus follow a lacto-vegetarian diet, so they consume dairy products but avoid meat and eggs. This is because Hinduism promotes *ahimsa* (non-violence) and many Hindus believe that abstaining from meat helps them practice this value.

- *Buddhism:* Some Buddhists follow a vegetarian or vegan diet, as the first of the Five Precepts (guidelines for ethical behavior) in Buddhism is to abstain from killing. However, this is not a universal requirement for all Buddhists, and some may choose to consume meat in moderation.

- *Jainism:* Jains follow a strict vegetarian diet that prohibits the consumption of meat, fish, eggs, and root vegetables, as these foods are believed to cause harm to living beings. Jains also practice ahimsa and believe in non-violence towards all living creatures.

- *Seventh-day Adventists:* Many Seventh-day Adventists follow a vegetarian or vegan diet, as the church promotes healthy living and believes in taking care of one's body as a temple of the Holy Spirit. However, this is not a requirement for all members of the church.

- *Hare Krishnas:* Members of the International Society for Krishna Consciousness, or Hare Krishnas, follow a lacto-vegetarian diet that excludes meat, fish, and eggs. This is because they believe that animals have souls and should not be harmed, and also because they believe that food prepared with a devotional attitude can enhance spiritual consciousness.

While vegetarianism is not a requirement in all religions, many religious traditions have dietary guidelines that encourage or require the consumption of plant-based foods and the avoidance of meat and animal products.

The Roman army rapidly built a vast network of roads throughout the Roman Empire using a combination of clever engineering techniques including surveying, leveling, and using multiple layers of materials to make their roads more durable.

The Romans built their roads in straight lines for several reasons, including efficiency of travel, ease of construction and maintenance, and military strategy.

The Roman army is famous for its impressive network of roads, which allowed the empire to connect its far-flung territories and move troops and goods quickly and efficiently. The Romans built their roads using a combination of engineering techniques, such as surveying to determine the best routes, leveling the ground to create a smooth surface, and constructing the road in multiple layers using materials such as gravel, sand, and paving stones.

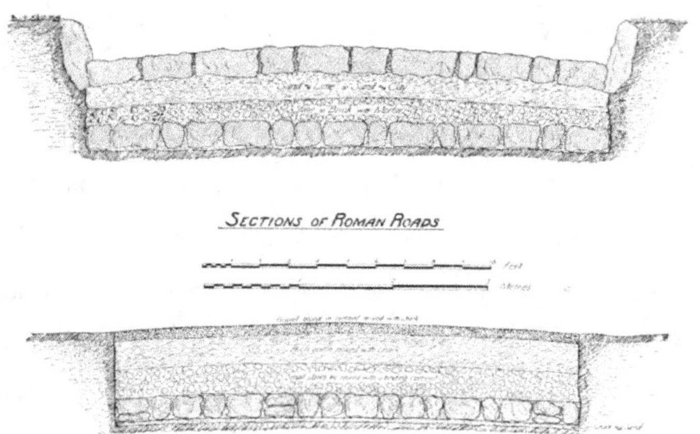

One of the key reasons the Romans built their roads in straight lines was for efficiency of travel. By creating a direct route from one place to another, the Romans could reduce travel time and make it easier for their armies and merchants to move from place to place. In addition, straight roads were easier to construct and maintain, as they required fewer turns and curves and could be built more quickly.

Another reason the Romans built their roads in straight lines was for military strategy. Straight roads allowed armies to move quickly and directly to their destinations, and made it easier to transport supplies and reinforcements. The Roman army also used their roads to control and monitor their territories, as they could move troops quickly to any part of the empire to put down rebellions or quell unrest.

Don't be fooled, though: Romans did not always build their roads in straight lines! They did sometimes follow field boundaries or other geographical features when it made sense to do so. But the majority of their roads were straight, as this allowed for greater efficiency and speed of travel.

34. WHAT WEAPONS AND ARMOR DID VIKING WARRIORS USE IN THE MIDDLE AGES?

Viking warriors used a variety of weapons and armor during the Middle Ages, including swords, axes, spears, and shields. They also wore protective clothing made of leather or chain mail.

Viking warriors were known for their fearsome reputation and their skilled use of weapons and armor. They typically carried swords, axes, and spears, as well as round shields made of wood and covered in animal hide or metal.

While Viking helmets were sometimes adorned with horns or wings, this is really a modern misconception as historical evidence suggests that they were usually much simpler in design.

Viking warriors also wore protective clothing made of leather or chain mail. This could include a helmet, a padded tunic, and leather or metal arm and leg guards. Some Vikings also carried bows and arrows, but these were less common than melee weapons.

While Vikings did engage in raiding and plundering during the Middle Ages, it is a myth that they simply burned down every town and village they encountered and stole everything valuable.

In reality, Viking raids were often targeted and strategic, aimed at capturing wealth and resources such as food, livestock, and precious metals.

Vikings were also known to establish trading relationships with some communities, and even settled in some areas to become farmers and traders themselves.

The Black Death or Bubonic Plague was a deadly disease which spread rapidly through Europe in the 14th century, likely through trade routes and human migration. The disease killed an estimated 30-60% of the European population.

To try to slow the spread of the disease, measures such as quarantine, isolation, and public health regulations were implemented, but these had limited effectiveness.

The Black Death was a pandemic that swept through Europe in the 14th century, killing millions of people. It is believed to have originated in Central Asia, and spread to Europe through trade routes and human migration. The disease was caused by the bacterium Yersinia pestis, which was transmitted by fleas that infested rats.

The Black Death spread so quickly through Europe because it was highly contagious and people did not understand how it was transmitted or how to treat it.

The disease could be transmitted through contact with infected people, contaminated objects, or the bites of infected fleas. This made it difficult to contain, and the lack of medical knowledge at the time meant that there was no effective treatment.

The Black Death had a devastating impact on the population of Europe, with an estimated 30-60% of the population dying from the disease. The mortality rate varied depending on factors such as age, health, and access to medical care, but it was particularly high in densely populated areas such as cities.

To try to slow the spread of the disease, various measures were implemented such as quarantine, isolation, and public health regulations. Quarantine involved isolating people who were suspected of having the disease, while isolation involved separating those who were known to be infected. Public health regulations such as sanitation measures and restrictions on public gatherings were also put in place, but these measures had limited effectiveness due to the lack of medical knowledge and the difficulty in enforcing them.

In the long term, the Black Death had far-reaching social and economic consequences, leading to changes in labor markets, the decline of feudalism, and the rise of the middle class.

Adding water to a dried-out seed can initiate the process of germination, which allows the seed to grow into a plant. In addition to water, most plants need nutrients such as nitrogen, phosphorus, and potassium, as well as sunlight and carbon dioxide, to grow and thrive.

Seeds are dormant until they receive the right conditions for germination, which includes sufficient moisture. When water is added to a dried-out seed, it triggers the seed to start taking up water through its outer coating, or seed coat. This initiates a series of chemical reactions that activate enzymes within the seed, which in turn break down stored nutrients such as starches and proteins. These nutrients are then converted into energy and building blocks for the growing plant.

In addition to water, most plants need other essential nutrients such as nitrogen, phosphorus, and potassium, which are often obtained from the soil. These nutrients are necessary for various processes in the plant, such as photosynthesis and the production of proteins and DNA. Some plants also require micronutrients such as iron, manganese, and zinc in smaller amounts.

Plants also need sunlight to carry out photosynthesis, which is the process by which they produce energy and food. Sunlight provides the energy that drives photosynthesis and is essential for the growth and development of most plants.

Lastly, plants need carbon dioxide, which is obtained from the air through tiny pores in their leaves called stomata. Carbon dioxide is used in photosynthesis to produce sugars and other organic compounds that the plant needs to grow and survive.

37. WHY DO SOME ANIMALS HAVE FUR AND OTHERS HAVE HAIR?

Some animals have fur and others have hair. The main difference between fur and hair is that fur is thicker, denser, and grows longer than hair.

Both fur and hair are made of keratin, a protein found in skin, hair, and nails. The main difference between them is the texture, length, and density of the strands.

Fur is typically thicker, denser, and grows longer than hair. It is also usually softer and more insulating, which makes it ideal for animals living in colder climates. Fur is usually shed seasonally, which allows animals to adapt to changing temperatures.

Hair, on the other hand, is thinner, grows

slower, and is less dense than fur. It covers most mammals, including humans, and serves a variety of purposes such as protecting the skin, regulating body temperature, and providing sensory information. Hair is also shed periodically, but not seasonally like fur.

While some animals have exclusively fur or hair, others have both. For example, dogs have fur on their bodies and hair on their ears, tails, and paws. Similarly, cats have fur all over their bodies but may have longer hairs on their tails or ears.

So why do some animals seem to molt (lose their fur) more than others? Animals molt to shed their old skin, feathers, or fur and replace them with new ones. The frequency of molting varies among different animal species and can be influenced by various factors.

One factor that can affect the frequency of molting is the animal's life cycle. For example, insects undergo a series of molts as they grow and develop from larvae to adult, and each molt is necessary for their growth and metamorphosis. In contrast, adult mammals typically molt their hair or fur only once or twice a year, usually in response to seasonal changes.

Another factor that can influence molting frequency is an animal's environment. Animals that live in harsh or extreme environments may need to molt more frequently to maintain their insulation or camouflage. For example, some Arctic animals have thick fur that they shed and replace each year to adapt to the changing climate.

Additionally, molting can be affected by an animal's diet and health. Animals that are malnourished or sick may molt more frequently as a result of stress or weakened immune systems.

38. CAN YOU LICK YOUR OWN ELBOW?

It is generally believed that it is impossible for most people to lick their own elbow due to anatomical limitations. However, there may be rare individuals who are able to do so if they have exceptional flexibility or a longer than average tongue.

The longest recorded human tongue was 3.97 inches (10.1 cm) from tip to top lip and belonged to a man named Nick Stoeberl from California, USA. Nick was officially recognized by the *Guinness World Records* in 2012 for having the world's longest tongue.

Believe it or not, it's also possible for some people to lick their own neck, but it depends on their individual anatomy and level of flexibility. People with longer necks, longer tongues, and more flexible spines have an easier time reaching their neck.

A raisin in fizzy lemonade floats up and down due to the carbon dioxide bubbles in the drink. When the lemonade is poured, the carbon dioxide gas in the liquid forms bubbles. These bubbles attach themselves to the rough surface of the raisin, causing it to float to the top of the liquid. Once the bubbles reach the surface of the liquid, they burst and the raisin loses its buoyancy, causing it to sink back down to the bottom.

The process then repeats itself again and again, making the raisin appear to float up and down in the fizzy lemonade.

Raisins don't release all the carbon dioxide in fizzy drinks like Mentos candies do because they don't have the same smooth and porous surface that Mentos have. Mentos candies have thousands of tiny pits on their surface that provide a nucleation site for the carbon dioxide bubbles to form and rapidly release. When Mentos are dropped into a carbonated beverage, these pits provide a massive amount of surface area for the carbon dioxide to rapidly form bubbles, causing a quick and explosive release of gas.

In contrast, raisins have a rough and uneven surface that provides far fewer nucleation sites for carbon dioxide bubbles to form. As a result, raisins release gas more slowly and less explosively than Mentos. However, because the surface of a raisin is still rough, it can create enough bubbles to make the raisin float up and down in a carbonated beverage, albeit at a slower rate than when Mentos are added.

40. DOES A VACUUM CLEANER REALLY MAKE A VACUUM?

No. A vacuum cleaner does not create a complete vacuum, but it does create a partial vacuum that is strong enough to pull in air and the dust and debris that it contains.

A vacuum cleaner works by using an electric motor to power a fan that draws air and debris into the vacuum through a nozzle or hose. As the air passes through the nozzle, it creates a low-pressure area that causes air from the surrounding environment to be sucked in.

As the air and debris enter the vacuum, they pass through a series of filters and collection chambers that separate the dirt and dust from the air. The first filter typically traps large particles like hair and dust bunnies, while subsequent filters trap smaller particles like pollen and allergens. Finally, in most modern vacuum cleaners, the air passes through a HEPA (high efficiency particulate air) filter, which captures tiny particles like pollens, bacteria and viruses.

To prevent dirt and dust from getting into the vacuum cleaner's motor, most vacuum cleaners use a system of filters and collection chambers to separate the dirt and debris from the air before it reaches the motor. This not only helps to protect the motor from damage, but it also ensures that the air that is expelled from the vacuum cleaner is clean and free of dust and other allergens.

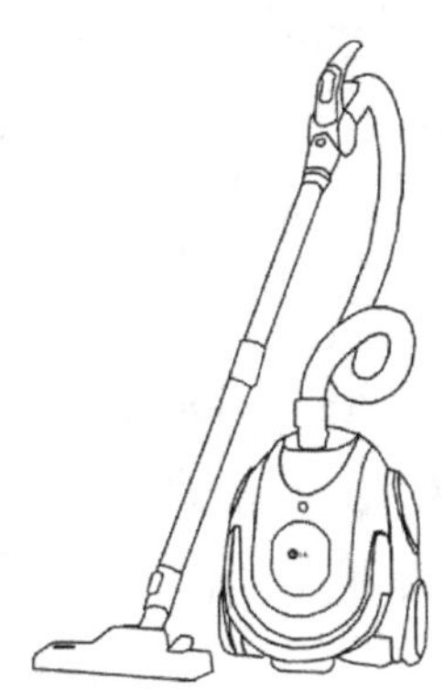

41. IS THERE A LIMIT TO HOW INTELLIGENT A HUMAN CAN BE?

There is no definitive limit to how intelligent a human can be, as intelligence is a complex and multifaceted trait that can manifest in many different ways. However, there are many factors that can influence a person's intelligence, including genetics, environment, and education.

IQ, or intelligence quotient, is a measure of a person's cognitive abilities, including reasoning, problem-solving, and critical thinking skills.

The highest recorded IQ score is 228, which was achieved by Marilyn vos Savant, an American woman who is best known for her column in Parade magazine, where she answers readers' questions on a wide range of topics.

But IQ tests are not a perfect measure of intelligence, and there is ongoing debate among scientists and psychologists about the validity and reliability of IQ tests as a measure of cognitive ability.

Additionally, there are many different types of intelligence that are not captured by traditional IQ tests, such as emotional intelligence, social intelligence, and creative intelligence.

Emotional Intelligence is the ability to recognize, understand, and manage one's own emotions and the emotions of others. It involves skills such as empathy, self-awareness, self-regulation, and social skills. Emotional intelligence can help individuals to communicate effectively, build positive relationships, and navigate social situations with sensitivity and awareness.

Social Intelligence refers to the ability to understand and navigate complex social situations, including social norms, customs, and expectations. It involves skills such as empathy, communication, social awareness, and the ability to read and interpret social cues. Social intelligence can help individuals to build strong social networks, negotiate social situations, and work effectively in group settings.

Creative Intelligence is the ability to think and innovate in novel and imaginative ways. It involves skills such as creativity, problem-solving, and innovation, and can be applied to a wide range of fields and domains. Creative intelligence can help individuals to come up with new ideas, solve complex problems, and create new products, services, and solutions.

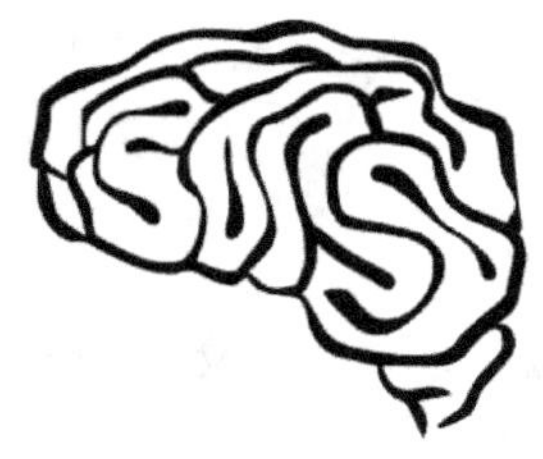

42. WHY DO WORDS LIKE 'MAYBE' START TO SOUND WEIRD IF YOU SAY THEM OVER AND OVER?

When words are repeated multiple times in quick succession, they can start to lose their meaning and become less familiar to the brain. This phenomenon is known as semantic satiation. As a result, the word "maybe" (or any other word) may begin to sound strange or unfamiliar if it is repeated too many times.

The brain's processing of language involves making connections between sounds and meanings. When we hear a word, our brains quickly recognize its meaning and associate it with other related concepts. However, when a word is repeated too many times, this process can become disrupted. The brain's connections between the sound and meaning of the word may become weaker or less efficient, leading to a sense of confusion or disorientation. So, saying the word "maybe" repeatedly may lead to a sense of unease or discomfort as the brain struggles to process the repeated sound and meaning.

Semantic satiation is a psychological phenomenon that occurs when a word is repeated many times in rapid succession, causing it to temporarily lose its meaning or become unfamiliar to the listener. The term was first coined in the 1960s by psychologist Leon Jakobovits James, who conducted a series of experiments to explore the effects of repeated exposure to words.

During semantic satiation, the repeated word may start to sound strange or even meaningless, as if it has been stripped of its usual associations and connotations. This can lead to a sense of disorientation or confusion, as the listener struggles to process the repeated sound without the usual contextual cues.

One theory behind semantic satiation is that it reflects a process of habituation or adaptation in the brain. When we are repeatedly exposed to a stimulus (in this case, a word), the brain may start to filter out the repetitive information in order to focus on more novel or salient stimuli. As a result, the repeated word may start to lose its impact or meaning, as the brain becomes less responsive to it.

Semantic satiation has been studied in a variety of contexts, including language processing, advertising, and cognitive psychology. It can be induced experimentally by asking participants to repeat a word out loud many times, or by presenting the word repeatedly in written form. It is an intriguing phenomenon that sheds light on the complex ways in which the brain processes language and stimuli from the environment.

It is difficult to identify a set of rules or laws that are common to all civilized societies because different societies have different legal systems and cultural norms. However, there are some fundamental principles that most societies agree on.

Among the most common rules observed by most civilized societies are:

1. Prohibitions on murder, theft, and other forms of violence against other people.

2. Respect for property rights and ownership.

3. Punishments for breaking the law, typically administered by a formal legal system.

4. The right to free speech, religion, and gathering together.

5. The need for a system of governance or leadership to enforce laws and maintain order.

These principles are typically viewed as necessary for maintaining social order and protecting the safety and well-being of individuals within a society. While the specific laws and customs of different societies may vary, these principles are generally considered to be essential for a society to be considered civilized.

Out of interest, most Western law is based on the now-extinct Latin language because it was the one used by ancient Romans, who created the first legal system that became the foundation of modern Western law. Latin was also the official language of the Catholic Church, which had significant influence on legal development in Europe during the Middle Ages. As a result, many legal terms and concepts have Latin roots and continue to be used in modern legal language.

The least amount of water you can drown in is about 2 teaspoons or 10 milliliters. Drowning occurs when someone's airway is blocked by liquid, usually water, and they can't breathe. This can lead to oxygen deprivation, brain damage, and eventually death.

It is possible to drown in other liquids like oil, alcohol, and even syrup, but water is the most common liquid people drown in.

There have been famous examples of dramatic drownings throughout history, such as the sinking of the Titanic, where over 1,500 people drowned in the frigid North Atlantic waters. Despite that, drowning is actually a relatively uncommon cause of death. (Even though a few high-profile celebrity deaths have raised awareness of the risks in recent years: Naya Rivera's sudden passing in 2020 shocked the world, and Mary Mara's accidental death in 2022 reminds us how easily it can happen. From rockstars to authors, there are a surprising number of celebrities who fell victim to drowning.)

So the big lesson is that everyone should learn to swim, and never forget that safety comes first whenever there's water nearby. If you're with your family or friends, everyone should be keeping an eye out for each other in case anyone gets into trouble in the water!

No, it's really not! The "five-second rule" is a popular belief that if you drop food on the floor and pick it up within five seconds, it's still safe to eat. However, studies have shown that bacteria and other harmful microorganisms can attach to the food almost immediately upon contact with a surface.

When food comes in contact with the floor or any other surface, it can pick up harmful bacteria and fungal spores that can cause foodborne illness. The amount of time it takes for this to happen depends on various factors such as the type of surface, the humidity, the temperature, and the moisture content of the food.

Research has shown that certain types of bacteria can transfer to food in less than a second, while other bacteria take longer to attach. For example, salmonella can attach to food in less than a second, while other bacteria like E. coli and staphylococcus can take several seconds to attach.

So I definitely wouldn't recommend eating food that has been dropped on the floor or any other surface, no matter how short a time it was there, to prevent the risk of foodborne illness!

The reason why people find other people's farts offensive but not their own is because we are more used to our own body odors, and also because we have a psychological association between our own farts and relief.

When we pass gas, our body releases a mixture of gases including nitrogen, oxygen, carbon dioxide, and methane. The unpleasant odor of farts comes from the small amount of hydrogen sulfide and other compounds that are released along with these gases. While the smell of our own farts may not be pleasant, we are more used to the smell because we have been exposed to it for our entire lives.

Another reason why we find other people's farts offensive is because of social norms and the fact that it is considered impolite or vulgar to fart in public. This cultural association with farting has made it a taboo subject that people are generally uncomfortable discussing.

As a result, there are many different words and phrases that people use instead of the word "fart". Some of these include "passing gas," "breaking wind," "guffing," "cutting the cheese," "letting one rip," "tooting," "trouser trumpet," "silent-but-deadlies," and many more besides! These phrases are often used in place of the word "fart" in order to avoid offending others, or for comic effect, or even to maintain a sense of decorum in certain social settings.

This phenomenon is known as "time contraction" or "time confabulation". It refers to the experience of checking the time and then immediately forgetting what the time was.

One explanation for this is that our brains prioritize new information over old information, and so when we check the time, our brains quickly process that information and then discard it in favor of more relevant information.

Another theory suggests that our brains don't encode the time into long-term memory because we don't see it as important or meaningful enough to remember.

In fact, quite often you're only checking the time either out of habit or to see if you've reached a particular time of day yet, so when your brain has finished deciding if the time is still important to you, it can just as quickly forget the time, knowing full well that you'll be checking it again soon anyway. Think about it: how often do you really need to know the exact time during a class, lecture, or meeting? All you really want to know is if it's nearly over yet, right?

Either way, the result is that we often forget what time it is immediately after checking our watch or phone. It's a common experience that most people have had at some point.

48. WHY DO SO MANY PEOPLE DIE SHORTLY AFTER RETIRING?

It's a horrible thought, but many families have had to deal with it. Sadly, some people die shortly after retiring thanks to a phenomenon known as the Retirement Death Syndrome. Several reasons have been suggested for this, including changes in lifestyle, loss of social connections, and loss of purpose.

Retirement can be a major life change, and it can have a significant impact on a person's physical and mental health. After retiring, some people may experience a loss of purpose, as they no longer have the same responsibilities and goals that they had while working. This can lead to feelings of boredom, depression, and anxiety, which can in turn lead to physical health problems such as high blood pressure, heart disease, and stroke.

Retirement can also lead to changes in lifestyle. People may become less active and spend more time sitting or lying down, which can increase the risk of obesity, diabetes, and other health problems. Additionally, retirement can lead to a loss of social connections, as people may no longer have daily interactions with coworkers and may become more isolated.

Don't worry though - it's not actually as common as many people seem to think! There haven't been many studies about retirement death syndrome, and there is no known percentage of retirees who die shortly after retiring. In fact, the idea that "many people die shortly after retiring" is a common misconception. While some limited studies have found a slightly higher mortality rate in the first year of retirement, it is not a common trend. Regardless, it's still absolutely essential to take care of your physical and mental health in retirement, including staying active, maintaining social connections, and seeking medical attention whenever necessary.

Sun exposure darkens your skin because it triggers the production of a pigment called melanin in your skin. However the Sun also lightens your hair because it breaks down the melanin that's already in your hair (which gives your hair its normal color), but individual hairs have no way of producing more melanin once they have already grown.

When you spend time in the sun, your skin gets darker because it produces more melanin. Melanin is a pigment that gives skin its color and protects it from UV radiation. The more time you spend in the sun, the more melanin your skin produces, and the darker your skin becomes.

However, the sun has the opposite effect on hair. Hair contains melanin too, but exposure to sunlight breaks down the melanin, causing the hair to become lighter. This is why people's hair often gets lighter in the summer, especially if they spend a lot of time outside.

Most importantly, prolonged sun exposure can be harmful to both the skin and hair, and can increase the risk of skin cancer and other health problems. It's always a good idea to protect your skin and hair from the sun by wearing sunscreen, hats, and other protective clothing.

When dry surfaces like rocks, stones or mosaics are exposed to clear water, their colors appear darker and more vivid. This is due to the change in light refraction caused by the water.

The reason why clear water can make dry surfaces appear darker and more colorful is related to the way light travels through water and air. Light moves slower through water than through air, and when it hits the surface of the water, some of it is reflected and some of it is refracted, or bent. This bending of light is what causes objects viewed through water to appear distorted.

When water is added to a dry surface, the light that hits it is refracted differently, making the colors appear more vivid and darker. This effect is especially noticeable on mosaics, where the addition of water can reveal details that were previously invisible. This is why archaeologists often wet mosaics when they are excavating them, to get a better idea of what they originally looked like.

However, this effect is only visible with clear water, as murky or dirty water can have the opposite effect and make colors appear more washed out.

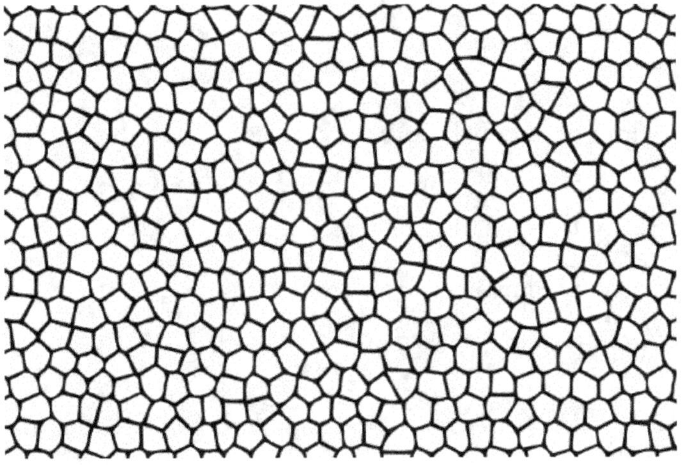

51. HOW DID NOTHING EXPLODE AND BECOME OUR WHOLE UNIVERSE?

The Big Bang theory explains the origin of the Universe. It suggests that the Universe began as a singularity, which is a point of infinite density and temperature. This singularity rapidly expanded and cooled, leading to the formation of all matter and energy that exist in the Universe today.

According to the Big Bang theory, there was no matter or energy before the singularity. In other words, there was nothing in the Universe as we know it. The singularity contained all the matter and energy that would eventually form the Universe, but in an extremely compressed and hot state.

As the Universe expanded, this matter and energy spread out, and the temperature and density decreased.

It is currently believed that the singularity was actually a single point of infinite density and temperature, where the laws of physics as we know them may not have applied. As the singularity expanded rapidly, it cooled and particles such as protons, neutrons, and electrons were able to form, eventually leading to the formation of atoms and, eventually, galaxies and stars.

The exact details of how the singularity formed and what caused it to expand are still being studied by scientists. However, observations of the cosmic microwave background radiation and the large-scale structure of the Universe support the Big Bang theory as the most plausible explanation for the origin of the Universe.

The Big Bang is estimated to have occurred about 13.8 billion years ago. This estimate is based on measurements of the cosmic microwave background radiation, which is the afterglow of the Big Bang, and other astronomical observations.

52. HOW DO HUMANS INSTINCTIVELY KNOW WHAT'S RIGHT AND WRONG?

It's entirely possible that we don't actually know right from wrong until we learn it from our parents and immediate environment.

There is no real agreement among scientists about whether humans have an in-built sense of right and wrong, or if moral beliefs are entirely shaped by cultural and environmental factors.

The question of whether humans have an innate sense of morality has been debated by philosophers and scientists for centuries.

Some argue that our moral beliefs are shaped by cultural and environmental factors, while others believe that there are universal moral principles that are hard-wired into our brains.

Recent studies suggest that humans may have an intuitive moral sense that is based on a few basic principles, such as fairness and harm avoidance, but these principles can also be influenced by cultural and social factors.

It's also worth noting that what one society considers "right" or "wrong" can vary significantly from another, which highlights the role of culture in shaping moral beliefs.

Ultimately, the question of whether humans have an innate sense of right and wrong remains a topic of ongoing debate and research.

53. HOW LONG DOES A HUMAN BODY TAKE TO DECOMPOSE AFTER BURIAL?

A human body can take a very long time - anything from six months to even hundreds of years - to decompose entirely into just a skeleton when buried in a wooden coffin, depending on various factors such as soil conditions, burial depth, and coffin quality.

After death, the decomposition process begins, and the body starts to break down. In a wooden coffin buried in the ground, the process can take anywhere from several months to several years to complete, depending on various factors. These factors include the quality of the coffin, the depth of the burial, the type of soil, and the climate.

In general, a body buried in a wooden coffin in moist soil will decompose more quickly than a body buried in dry soil. The coffin can also affect the rate of decomposition, as a well-sealed coffin will slow down the process, while a poorly sealed one will allow more air and moisture to enter, speeding up the process.

In ideal conditions, a body can take around 10-12 years to decompose entirely into just a skeleton. Depending on all the factors involved, however, it could take as little as six months for a body to decompose, while in other cases it may take several decades or even centuries.

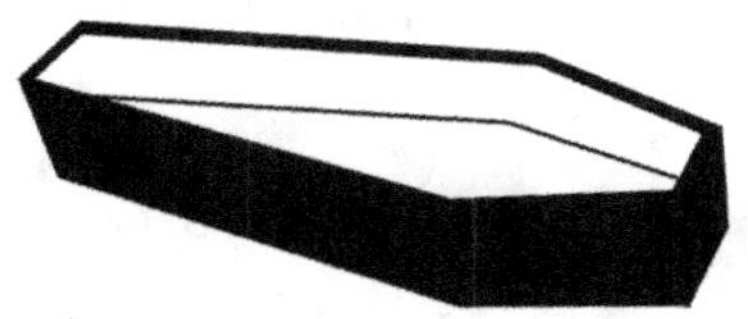

If all the ships and boats in the world were to disappear at once, the sea level would drop by a very small amount - perhaps 0.01 of a millimeter.

The displacement of water caused by ships and boats floating on the ocean's surface is relatively small compared to the vast volume of the world's oceans.

The total displacement of all the ships and boats in the world is estimated to be around 1.2 billion cubic meters, which seems like a large number, but it is only a tiny fraction of the ocean's overall volume.

Therefore, if all the ships and boats were to disappear at once, the sea level would drop by a negligible amount, approximately 0.01 millimeters, which is too small to be noticeable.

But don't worry... It is highly unlikely that all boats in the world would sink at the same time without any external force acting upon them. Natural disasters like tsunamis or storms could cause widespread damage to boats, but it is still unlikely that all boats would sink at once. A hypothetical scenario that could cause all boats to sink simultaneously would be a massive electromagnetic pulse (EMP) that could disrupt electronic systems on boats and cause them to malfunction or sink. However, this is incredibly unlikely to actually happen!

There's obviously no exact answer to this because the amount of food and liquid a person consumes in their lifetime will vary according to gender, general health, and lifestyle. However, estimates suggest that an average person will get through at least 16,000 kilograms of food and more than 58,000 liters of liquid!

Let's break down the math behind those estimates. If we assume that the average human consumes around 2,000 kilocalories (kcal) per day, and we assume an average lifespan of 80 years, the total number of days a person would live is:

$$80 \times 365 = 29,200 \text{ days}$$

So the total number of calories consumed by the average human being during their entire lifetime would be approximately:

$$2,000 \text{ kcal/day} \times 29,200 \text{ days}$$

$$= 58,400,000 \text{ kcal}$$

Next, to convert this into theoretical kilograms of food, we need to know the average calorie density of food. Let's assume it is around 3.5 kcal/gram. So, the total amount of food consumed would be:

$$58,400,000 \text{ kcal} / 3.5 \text{ kcal/gram}$$

$$= \textbf{16,686 kilograms} \text{ in a lifetime}$$

But what about the liquids? The average human drinks around 2 liters of liquid per day. Using the same lifespan of 80 years, the total amount of liquid consumed in a lifetime would be:

$$2 \text{ liters/day} \times 29,200 \text{ days}$$

$$= \textbf{58,400 liters}$$

So the average human would consume approximately 58,400 liters of liquid in their lifetime.

Fish cannot get seasick as they do not have a vestibular system, which is responsible for motion sickness in humans. They have a specialized organ called the otolith, which allows them to determine their orientation in the water.

In humans, seasickness (also known as motion sickness) is caused by a conflict between the senses. The inner ear's vestibular system, which is responsible for balance, detects motion while the eyes are focused on a stationary object such as the interior of a boat's cabin. This sensory conflict sends mixed signals to the brain, which can result in nausea, dizziness, and other unpleasant symptoms.

But it's not just on the sea that you get seasick; It can be experienced while traveling by boat, car, plane or on just about any other vehicle.

In a fish, the otolith is a small calcium carbonate structure located in the fish's inner ear. The otolith detects changes in the fish's acceleration and helps them determine which way is "up" toward the surface of the water and which way is "down" toward the bottom.

The otolith works by detecting the movement of small stones within the fish's inner ear as the fish accelerates or decelerates.

The movement of the stones signals to the fish which way is "up" and which way is "down" relative to the water's surface. This allows them to maintain their balance and orientation in the water, even in turbulent conditions.

57. WHY DOESN'T LIQUID GLUE STICK TO THE INSIDE OF THE BOTTLE?

When liquid glue is inside the bottle, it is not exposed to air. Glue requires air to dry and harden. So, when the glue is inside the bottle, it doesn't have access to air and doesn't dry out or harden.

Different types of glue have different chemical compositions, which affect how they dry and set. Some glues contain solvents, which evaporate as the glue dries. The rate at which the solvents evaporate can affect how quickly the glue dries. Other factors that can affect the drying time include temperature, humidity, and the thickness of the glue layer. Some glues may also require a chemical reaction to occur for them to dry and set, which can take longer than just drying out.

No, you can't yawn while you're asleep.

Yawning is a reflex that occurs when you take a deep breath in and then exhale. When you are asleep, your body is in a relaxed state, and your breathing is slower and more regular. That's why it's not possible. If you yawn, you're definitely awake.

Okay, so if you can't yawn while you're asleep, can you dream without actually falling asleep? Again the answer is a big fat 'no' - you can't dream without actually falling asleep. In other words, what people call 'day dreaming' is not actually dreaming!

Dreams occur during the Rapid Eye Movement (REM) stage of sleep, which is one of the four stages of the sleep cycle. During REM sleep, your brain is highly active, and you experience vivid dreams. If you are not asleep, you cannot enter the REM stage of sleep and, therefore, cannot dream. Daydreaming or imagining things while awake is not the same as dreaming during sleep.

How does sleep actually work?

There are four different stages of sleep that a person goes through during a complete sleep cycle. These stages are:

Stage 1: Light Sleep

This is the lightest stage of sleep, where you are just drifting off to sleep. During this stage, you may experience a feeling of floating, and your muscles may twitch. Your brain produces alpha and theta waves during this stage.

Stage 2: Core Sleep

This stage is characterized by a slightly deeper sleep than stage 1. Your heart rate and breathing slow down, and your body temperature drops. Your brain produces theta waves with brief bursts of higher-frequency brain waves called sleep spindles.

Stage 3: Deep Sleep

This is the deep sleep stage, also known as slow-wave sleep. During this stage, your brain produces delta waves, and it is difficult to wake you up. Your breathing and heart rate are at their lowest during this stage.

Stage 4: REM Sleep

The REM (Rapid Eye Movement) sleep stage is called REM because your eyes move rapidly back and forth during this stage. This is when you experience vivid dreams, and your brain is very active. Your heart rate and breathing increase, and your muscles become paralyzed to prevent you from acting out your dreams.

The sleep cycle repeats itself multiple times throughout the night, with each cycle lasting about 90-120 minutes. As the night progresses, the time spent in deep sleep decreases, while the time spent in REM sleep increases.

59. IF YOU OWN A PIECE OF LAND, HOW FAR DOWN AND HOW FAR UP DO YOU OWN IT?

As a landowner, you own the land from the surface to the center of the Earth and from the surface up to the airspace above your land. However, the extent of your ownership may be limited by laws and regulations in your area.

The concept of land ownership includes what is called "subsurface rights" and "airspace rights." Subsurface rights refer to everything beneath the surface of the land, including minerals, oil, and gas. Airspace rights refer to the space above the land, including the right to build structures and fly aircraft.

However, the extent of these rights can be limited by laws and regulations. For example, some areas may have restrictions on drilling for resources beneath the surface of the land, or building structures that are too tall and encroach on the airspace of neighboring properties.

The rules and regulations surrounding land ownership are typically decided by the government or local authorities, such as zoning boards, city councils, or state legislatures. These regulations are put in place to ensure that land use is consistent with community values and public safety.

60. IS IT POSSIBLE TO BE ALLERGIC TO TAP WATER?

Yes... and no. It's impossible to be allergic to pure water itself, but some people do have a sensitivity to the chemicals, minerals, or bacteria that are present in tap water, which can cause skin irritation, itching, or rashes. This sensitivity is not the same as an allergic reaction.

If you are experiencing skin irritation or other symptoms when using tap water, there are several things you can do. First, you can try filtering your tap water to remove any impurities that may be causing your symptoms. You can also try using a different type of soap or detergent when washing with tap water.

In some cases, installing a water softener or water filter in your home may also help. But if your symptoms persist, you should definitely see a doctor to rule out any underlying medical conditions that may be causing your symptoms. They may also recommend using topical creams or medications to relieve your symptoms.

Overall, it is important to remember that tap water is generally safe to use and drink, and any sensitivity or irritation is usually a minor issue that can be addressed with simple solutions.

61. WHAT IS THE CORRECT WAY TO BRUSH YOUR TEETH?

The correct way to brush your teeth is to use a fluoride toothpaste and brush for at least two minutes, twice a day. It's important to brush all surfaces of your teeth, including the front, back, and chewing surfaces, and to use gentle circular motions.

After brushing, you should spit the toothpaste out into the sink. It's not necessary to rinse your mouth out with water immediately after spitting. In fact, it's better to wait for a few minutes before rinsing, as this allows the fluoride in the toothpaste to stay on your teeth and continue protecting them.

When you do rinse your mouth out with water, make sure to use a small amount and swish it around your mouth for a few seconds before spitting it out. Don't use too much water, as this can wash away the fluoride from the toothpaste and reduce its effectiveness.

So what is Fluoride and how does it protect your teeth? Well, it's important to have it in your toothpaste because it helps to prevent tooth decay and cavities. When you eat sugary or starchy foods, the bacteria in your mouth produce acid that can erode the enamel on your teeth, leading to cavities. Fluoride works by strengthening the enamel on your teeth, making it more resistant to acid erosion.

Fluoride also has a remineralizing effect on your teeth, meaning that it can help to repair early stages of tooth decay before a cavity forms. It does this by promoting the remineralization of areas of your teeth that have been weakened by acid.

In addition to being in toothpaste, fluoride is also commonly added to public water supplies to help protect people's teeth. This practice, called water fluoridation, has been shown to be a safe and effective way to improve oral health and prevent tooth decay.

It's important to use fluoride toothpaste as part of a regular oral hygiene routine, along with brushing twice a day and flossing daily, to maintain good dental health and prevent cavities. However, it's also important not to swallow toothpaste, as ingesting too much fluoride can be harmful.

62. WHY DON'T ARM AND LEG HAIRS GET 'SPLIT ENDS'?

Arm and leg hairs don't get split ends because they have a different structure than the hairs on your head.

The main difference is that arm and leg hairs are vellus hairs, which are short, fine, and not pigmented, while the hairs on your head are terminal hairs, which are longer, thicker, and pigmented.

Vellus hairs don't have a medulla, which is the innermost layer of a hair shaft, and they also have a smaller diameter than terminal hairs. Split ends occur when the cuticle, which is the outermost layer of a hair shaft, becomes damaged and starts to peel away from the hair. Because vellus hairs don't have a medulla and have a smaller diameter, they are less likely to become damaged in this way.

In addition to the structural differences, the growth cycles of arm and leg hairs and head hairs also differ. Arm and leg hairs have a shorter growth cycle and a smaller growth phase than head hairs. This means that arm and leg hairs don't grow as long or as quickly as head hairs.

So, the main difference between arm hairs and the hairs on your head is their structure and growth cycle. Arm and leg hairs are vellus hairs, which are shorter, finer, and less likely to get split ends than the terminal hairs on your head.

*I know what you're thinking. But no, the light from your headlights would **not** travel faster than the speed of light. According to the theory of relativity, nothing can travel faster than the speed of light.*

This means that even if the car was able to travel at the speed of light, the light from the headlights would still travel at the same speed relative to the car and would not exceed the speed of light.

But of course, as the car approaches the speed of light, the energy required to accelerate it further increases infinitely. This means that it is not possible for any object with mass to actually reach the speed of light.

Even in a hypothetical scenario where a car could travel at the speed of light, the light from its headlights would still travel at the speed of light relative to the car and would not exceed this limit.

Out of interest, the Speed of Light is a fundamental physical constant (known simply as 'C') that represents the speed at which light travels in a vacuum. It is approximately 299,792,458 meters per second, or about 186,282 miles per second.

The first accurate measurement of the speed of light was made by the Danish astronomer Ole Rømer in the late 17th century. Rømer was studying the moons of Jupiter and noticed that their eclipses appeared to occur at different times depending on the position of Earth in its orbit around the Sun. He correctly deduced that this was due to the varying distance between Earth and Jupiter, and used this information to calculate the speed of light.

However, it wasn't until the 19th century that the speed of light was measured with greater accuracy. In 1849, the French physicist Hippolyte Fizeau used a rapidly rotating toothed wheel to measure the speed of light, and later in the century, the American physicist Albert Michelson used an interferometer to make even more precise measurements.

Today, the speed of light is a crucial component of many areas of physics, including relativity, quantum mechanics, and electromagnetism. It is also used in practical applications such as telecommunications and astronomy, where the speed of light is used to measure distances in space.

Having one big time zone for the entire world is not practical because the Earth is divided into 24 time zones, each approximately 15 degrees of longitude wide, with each zone having roughly the same hours of daylight as other time zones (thanks to the Earth's steady rotation throughout the day).

Each time zone represents a different hour of the day and helps to synchronize time across regions. Without time zones, it would be very difficult to coordinate events, transportation, and communication across the globe.

As for Daylight Savings Time (DST), it is a practice where people adjust their clocks forward by one hour during the summer months to make better use of the longer daylight hours. The idea is to move an hour of daylight from the morning to the evening, which can save energy and make it easier to engage in outdoor activities. DST is not universally observed, however, and some countries do not use it at all, while others have used it in the past but have since discontinued the practice.

The decision to use DST is usually made by individual countries or regions based on their own preferences and needs. Some argue that DST is not necessary in areas close to the equator where the length of daylight remains relatively constant throughout the year. Others believe that DST can disrupt sleep patterns and cause other health problems, while some see it as an important tool for conserving energy and promoting outdoor activities.

Because of all the different countries, environments and people involved, this particular debate will probably never end.

65. HOW AND WHY DO SHEEP AND COWS SLEEP STANDING UP?

Sheep and cows have a strange ability to sleep while standing up because they have a special arrangement of bones and muscles in their legs that allows them to lock their joints and maintain a standing position without using too much energy.

This is clearly an evolutionary adaptation that allows them to rest and sleep while staying alert and ready to flee from potential predators.

While sheep and cows are perhaps the most well-known animals that can sleep standing up, there are other species that are also capable of this feat.

Horses, for example, are able to sleep standing up using a similar mechanism as sheep and cows.

Some birds, such as flamingos and some species of ducks, also sleep standing on one leg, which allows them to conserve heat while sleeping in cold environments.

Out of interest, there are also some animals (not just bats) that sleep upside down! They include bats, yes, but also sloths and some of the primates.

Bats are known for their ability to sleep hanging upside down from trees or caves, which allows them to quickly fly away if needed.

Sloths also sleep upside down, hanging from branches with their long, curved claws, which help them to stay attached to the tree.

Some primates, such as orangutans and gibbons, also sleep while hanging upside down from trees, using their strong arms to maintain their position.

Worms are a common type of invertebrate that can be found in many parts of the world. While some people may find the idea of eating worms unappealing, they are actually a source of protein and other nutrients in many cultures.

The taste of worms can vary depending on the species and how they are prepared. Some people describe the taste as similar to chicken or fish, while others find the texture and flavor unappealing. In general, worms are not commonly eaten in Western cultures, but they are considered a delicacy in some parts of the world.

In many Asian countries, for example, various types of worms are consumed as snacks or as part of a meal. In China, for instance, fried silk worms are a popular street food, while in Thailand, bamboo worms are often eaten fried or roasted. In some African countries, termites and other insects are also consumed for their nutritional value.

It is important to note, however, that not all types of worms are safe to eat. Some species can be toxic or carry parasites that can be harmful to humans. It is therefore important to only consume worms that have been properly prepared and sourced from reputable suppliers.

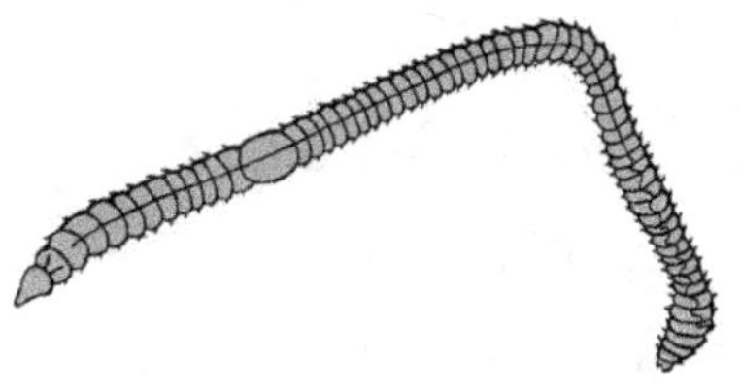

Farts and burps are both natural bodily functions that occur as a result of the digestive process. They're nothing to be embarrassed about, either - everybody does them!

Farts are caused by the buildup of gas in the intestines, which is then expelled through the rectum. Burps, on the other hand, are caused by the release of gas from the stomach through the mouth.

Certain foods and drinks are more likely to cause gas buildup in the digestive system, leading to more frequent burping and farting. Foods that are high in fiber, such as beans, whole grains, and certain vegetables, can be particularly problematic for some people. Dairy products, fatty foods, and carbonated drinks can also contribute to gas buildup.

To reduce the likelihood of farting or burping, it can be helpful to avoid or limit certain foods and drinks that are known to cause gas. Eating smaller, more frequent meals can also help to reduce gas buildup in the digestive system. Additionally, taking time to chew food thoroughly and avoiding talking while eating can help to reduce the amount of air that is swallowed during meals.

If excessive farting or burping is a persistent problem, it may be a sign of an underlying digestive issue or food intolerance. It is important to talk to a healthcare provider if symptoms persist or are accompanied by other symptoms such as abdominal pain, bloating, or changes in bowel habits.

Thoughts are complex mental processes that involve the brain processing and interpreting sensory information, memories, and emotions. They can be influenced by external factors such as experiences, interactions with others, and environmental cues.

While it is difficult to determine whether any thoughts are truly original, it is likely that most thoughts are a combination of previous experiences and learned information. The brain has the ability to process and integrate multiple pieces of information to form new ideas and concepts.

The process of generating new ideas can involve the combination and reorganization of existing knowledge and experiences in novel ways. This can occur through various cognitive processes such as attention, perception, memory, and language. The brain can also make use of problem-solving strategies and creative thinking techniques to generate new ideas.

Recent studies have shown that the brain can create new connections and neural pathways through experiences and learning, which can lead to the generation of new thoughts and ideas. These new connections can facilitate creative thinking and problem-solving abilities.

So now you know... thoughts are a complex product of the brain's processing of sensory information, memories, and emotions. While many thoughts are likely a combination of previous experiences and learned information, the brain has the ability to generate new ideas by reorganizing existing knowledge and making new connections.

69. HOW OLD ARE HUMAN BABIES WHEN THEY LEARN TO RESPOND TO THEIR NAME?

Human babies typically learn to respond to their name between 4-7 months of age. On average, a human baby will learn its first 100 words between 12-18 months of age.

Responding to their name is one of the earliest communication milestones for infants. By 4-7 months, most babies are able to recognize their own name and turn their heads in the direction of the sound. This ability is crucial for developing social skills and forming bonds with caregivers.

Learning language is a more complex process and typically takes longer. While there is variability between individual babies, research has found that on average, babies will begin to say their first words around 12 months of age. By 18 months, most babies will have a vocabulary of around 50 words, and by 24 months, around 200-300 words.

It's important to note that language development is influenced by a range of factors, including genetics, environment, and social interactions. Some babies may learn words earlier or later than average, and some may have delays or disorders that affect their language development.

Caregivers can support language development by talking to and interacting with their babies regularly, and seeking professional help if they have concerns about their child's language development.

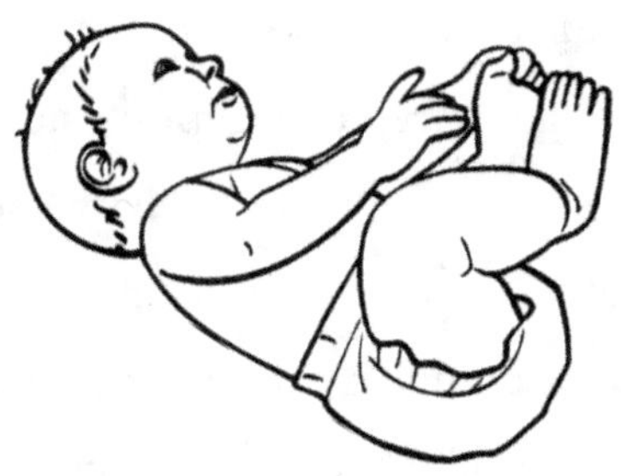

70. HOW CAN WE PROVE WE'RE NOT LIVING IN A BIG COMPUTER SIMULATION?

The question of whether we are living in a computer simulation is a philosophical and scientific debate that has been ongoing for years. There is no conclusive evidence to prove or disprove the idea that we are living in a simulated reality. While some argue that it can't be ruled out, most find the theory quite unlikely.

The argument that we might be living in a computer simulation is based on the premise that a technologically advanced civilization, such as our own, could create a simulated universe that is indistinguishable from the real one. In this scenario, everything we see and experience could be part of a complex virtual reality program, much like the world depicted in the movie "The Matrix."

Those who believe that we might be living in a simulation point to the rapid advances in technology and the fact that we are already creating virtual worlds that are becoming more realistic and immersive. They also argue that there are limits to what we can observe and know about the universe, and that we might be limited by the constraints of the simulation.

On the other hand, many experts in science and philosophy find the theory of a computer simulation unlikely. They argue that the idea is based on speculation and lacks empirical evidence. Additionally, there is no reason to believe that a civilization would have the resources or motivation to create such a complex simulation.

While the question of whether we are living in a computer simulation remains unanswered, many scientists and philosophers believe that it is ultimately unimportant. Whether we are living in a simulation or not, the reality that we experience is the only one that matters to us, and we must make the most of it.

71. HOW MANY DIFFERENT WAYS ARE THERE TO WIN AT NAUGHTS AND CROSSES?

There are 255,168 possible different game patterns on a Naughts And Crosses (also known as Tic-Tac-Toe). And going first definitely gives you an advantage... The first player generally wins 131,184 of the possible combinations, while the second player wins only 77,904 games, and the remaining 46,080 will be a draw anyway.

Naughts and Crosses is a two-player game played on a 3x3 grid. The objective is to get three of your symbol (either naughts or crosses) in a row, either horizontally, vertically, or diagonally.

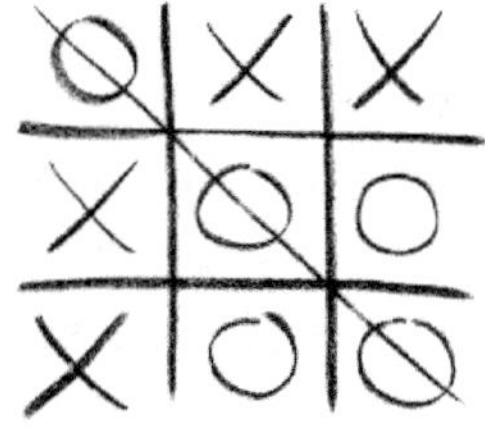

If well-played, with some reasonable strategy to them, most games will be a draw. To see why, imagine that the first player chooses a corner as their first move. The second player must then choose a side square, as choosing another corner would give the first player a win.

This limits the available moves, and eventually leads to a draw if both players play perfectly, because the game is simple enough that a perfect strategy can be developed. In fact, it is mathematically proven that if both players play perfectly, the game will always end in a draw.

72. WHY DO WE SEE BIG FIREWORKS SPARKLE BEFORE WE HEAR THE BANG?

When watching fireworks, we often see the sparks and colors before we hear the loud bang because light travels faster than sound. We can estimate the distance of a firework or lightning flash by counting the number of seconds between seeing the flash and hearing the sound, and multiplying by the speed of sound.

The reason we see the visual effects of fireworks before hearing the sound is due to the difference in speed between light and sound. Light travels much faster than sound, at a speed of approximately 299,792,458 meters per second in a vacuum. In comparison, sound travels at a much slower speed of approximately 343 meters per second in air.

When a firework explodes, the light travels much faster than the sound waves it creates. The light reaches our eyes almost instantly, while the sound waves take longer to reach our ears. This creates a delay between seeing the explosion and hearing the sound.

Similarly, with lightning, the light travels much faster than the sound waves it creates. We see the lightning flash almost instantly, while the sound waves take longer to reach us. By counting the number of seconds between seeing the lightning and hearing the thunder, we can estimate the distance of the lightning strike.

To estimate the distance of a firework or lightning flash, we can use the fact that sound travels at a constant speed in air. The speed of sound in air is approximately 343 meters per second at room temperature and normal atmospheric pressure. To estimate the distance of a firework or lightning strike, we can count the number of seconds between seeing the flash and hearing the sound, and multiply this number by 343 to get the rough distance in meters.

For example, if we see a firework explode and hear the sound 5 seconds later, the distance of the firework would be approximately 1715 meters (5 seconds x 343 meters per second). This method is not exact, as the speed of sound can be affected by temperature, humidity, and other factors. However, it can provide a rough estimate of the distance of a distant object without the need for a stopwatch or timer.

There is no evidence to support the claim that the first NASA Moon landing was faked, and a wealth of evidence exists to confirm its authenticity.

Theories that suggest the Moon landing was faked often rely on misunderstandings or misrepresentations of scientific principles or evidence. Theories that support the Moon landing's authenticity point to the vast amount of scientific data and physical evidence that has been gathered by NASA and independent researchers.

The first NASA Moon landing occurred on July 20, 1969, when the Apollo 11 mission successfully landed two astronauts, Neil Armstrong and Edwin "Buzz" Aldrin, on the Moon's surface. Despite the overwhelming evidence that supports the authenticity of the Moon landing, there are still some who believe that it was faked. These theories often rely on misunderstandings or misrepresentations of scientific principles or evidence.

One theory that suggests the Moon landing was faked is that the American flag planted on the Moon appears to be waving in the wind, despite the Moon having no atmosphere. However, this is simply an optical illusion caused by the flag's movement as it was being planted, and has been debunked by NASA scientists.

Another theory is that the shadows in the Moon landing photographs appear to be inconsistent, suggesting that they were filmed in a studio with artificial lighting. However, the inconsistencies in the shadows can be explained by the uneven terrain and the angle of the Sun's light, and have been demonstrated by NASA scientists and independent researchers.

Theories that support the Moon landing's authenticity point to the vast amount of scientific data and physical evidence that has been gathered by NASA and independent researchers. The Lunar Reconnaissance Orbiter, for example, has taken high-resolution photographs of the Moon's surface that show the landing sites and the tracks left by the astronauts. Additionally, the Apollo missions returned hundreds of kilograms of Moon rocks that have been extensively studied and analyzed by scientists.

So, the vast majority of evidence supports the authenticity of the first NASA Moon landing, and there is no credible evidence to suggest that it was faked. The theories that suggest the Moon landing was faked often rely on misunderstandings or misrepresentations of scientific principles or evidence, and have been thoroughly debunked by NASA scientists and independent researchers.

74. HOW MANY ENGLISH WORDS ARE THERE, AND HOW DOES AN ADULT KNOW?

The number of English words is difficult to determine due to the language's constantly evolving nature and the inclusion of new words. However, estimates suggest that there are between 170,000 and 250,000 words in current use in the English language. The average adult knows 20,000 to 35,000 of them.

The English language is constantly evolving and changing, with new words being added and old words falling out of use. As a result, it is difficult to determine the exact number of words in the language.

Estimates of the number of words in English vary widely, with some suggesting there are around 170,000 words in current use, while others put the number at closer to 250,000.

One of the challenges in determining the number of English words is that many words can have multiple meanings, and the meanings of words can change over time. This can make it difficult to draw clear boundaries between different words and to determine what should be considered a separate word.

Despite the challenges in determining the number of English words, it is possible to estimate the number of words that an average adult knows. Studies have shown that the average adult native speaker of English knows between 20,000 and 35,000 words. However, this number can vary depending on factors such as education level, occupation, and personal interests.

It is also worth noting that knowing a word does not necessarily mean being able to define it or use it correctly in all contexts. Vocabulary knowledge is complex and multi-dimensional, and includes aspects such as knowledge of word meanings, pronunciation, spelling, and usage.

It isn't possible to be absolutely sure that the way we see colors is exactly the same as other people, as it is a subjective experience. However, we can assume that our perception of colors is similar based on the fact that we all have the same types of color receptors in our eyes and the same neural pathways for processing color information.

Color perception is a subjective experience that is influenced by many factors, including genetics, environmental factors, and individual differences in perception.

So while it is impossible to know for certain that we all see colors the same way, we can assume that our perception of colors is similar based on the fact that we all have the same types of color receptors in our eyes and the same neural pathways for processing color information.

The human eye contains three types of color receptors, known as cones, that are responsible for detecting color. Each cone is most sensitive to a particular range of wavelengths of light, which correspond to the colors red, green, and blue. The brain then combines the signals from the cones to create the perception of color. While there can be individual variations in the sensitivity of each type of cone, the underlying mechanisms of color vision are the same for all humans.

Despite these similarities, there can still be differences in the way that individuals perceive colors. For example, some people are colorblind, meaning they have a genetic variation that affects the function of one or more types of cones, resulting in a reduced ability to distinguish certain colors.

Additionally, individual differences in perception can result in different interpretations of the same color, such as whether a particular shade of blue is more green or more purple.

While there is no experiment that can definitively prove that we all see colors the same way, there are tests that can provide some insights into differences in color perception among individuals. For example, color blindness tests use patterns of colored dots or lines to test an individual's ability to distinguish between different colors. Other tests, such as the Ishihara color plates, use images of colored dots to test for various types of colorblindness.

Are you really **you?**

Am I really **me?**

The idea that your own existence is the only certainty, and everything else may be imaginary, is called solipsism. Solipsism is a branch of philosophy that argues that one can only be certain of their own existence and everything else is uncertain.

Solipsism is a highly debated philosophical theory that argues that only the self is real and all else, including other people and the external world, is only a product of the mind. This means that there is no objective reality outside of the individual's mind, and all external experiences are simply constructions of the mind.

Some people might believe in solipsism because they find it difficult to believe that they can truly know anything outside of their own subjective experiences. Solipsism can also appeal to people who find comfort in the idea that they are in complete control of their own reality and that they alone create their own experiences. Furthermore, some people may be drawn to solipsism as a way of dealing with mental health issues, such as anxiety or depression, by retreating into an imaginary world where they can have complete control.

However, many philosophers and scientists reject solipsism as an overly simplistic and unfalsifiable theory. They argue that the existence of other minds and the external world can be inferred through empirical evidence and logical reasoning. For example, people can observe others' behavior and infer that they have thoughts and feelings similar to their own. Additionally, science has developed a number of methods to test and validate claims about the external world, which confirm that the external world exists in its own right.

If all the electricity grids in the world failed at once due to a massive electromagnetic pulse from the Sun, it would have catastrophic consequences for human civilization. The short answer is that some humans would likely survive, but the impact would be devastating.

Electromagnetic pulses (EMPs) are intense bursts of electromagnetic energy that can occur naturally, such as from a solar storm, or through human-made devices, such as nuclear weapons.

An EMP from the Sun could potentially disrupt or destroy electronic equipment, including the electricity grids that power modern civilization.

The loss of electricity would have immediate and widespread consequences. Without electricity, many essential services would be disrupted, such as water and sewage treatment, medical facilities, and transportation systems. This would lead to widespread illness, death, and social unrest.

Furthermore, the loss of electricity would impact food production and distribution, as modern agriculture relies heavily on electricity for irrigation, refrigeration, and transportation. This could lead to famine and food shortages.

Despite the catastrophic consequences, some humans would likely survive. Those who live in rural areas and have skills for self-sufficiency, such as farming and hunting, would have a better chance of survival. Additionally, those who have preparedness plans and supplies, such as food, water, and shelter, would be more likely to survive.

78. DID GEORGE WASHINGTON REALLY HAVE WOODEN TEETH?

The common belief that George Washington had wooden teeth is a myth. Washington did wear false teeth, but they were not made of wood. Instead, his dentures were made from a combination of materials, including human and animal teeth, ivory, and metal.

George Washington suffered from dental problems throughout his life, likely due to poor dental hygiene and dietary habits. By the time he became president, he had lost most of his teeth and had difficulty eating and speaking.

Washington's first set of dentures, made when he was in his 20s, were constructed from human teeth, which were commonly used in dentures at the time. Over the years, he had several sets of dentures made, each one slightly different in design and materials. Some of his later dentures contained animal teeth, such as those from horses and cows, as well as ivory and metal springs.

Despite the variety of materials used, Washington's dentures were reportedly uncomfortable and ill-fitting. He often complained of pain and difficulty speaking while wearing them. While his dentures were an important part of his daily life, they were reportedly uncomfortable and caused him significant discomfort.

79. DOES COOKING WITH WINE MAKE THE FOOD ALCOHOLIC?

When cooking with wine, the alcohol content does not entirely boil off. However, the amount of alcohol remaining in the dish depends on various factors such as the cooking time, method, and temperature. In most cases, only a small percentage of the alcohol content will remain.

The amount of alcohol remaining in a dish depends on several factors, including the amount of wine used and the length of time it is cooked. If wine is added to a dish and immediately removed from heat, it will retain most of its alcohol content. However, if the dish is simmered for an extended period, the alcohol content will decrease over time.

According to a study by the U.S. Department of Agriculture, the alcohol content in a dish decreases as follows:

- 85% of the alcohol remains after 15 minutes of cooking

- 70% of the alcohol remains after 30 minutes of cooking

- 45% of the alcohol remains after 1 hour of cooking

- 25% of the alcohol remains after 2 hours of cooking

- 10% of the alcohol remains after 3 hours of cooking

It is worth noting that the alcohol content in a dish will never reach zero, as some alcohol will always remain. However, the amount of alcohol remaining is typically small enough that it would not make the food alcoholic.

In conclusion, cooking with wine does not make the food alcoholic, as only a small percentage of the alcohol content remains after cooking. The amount of alcohol remaining in the dish depends on various factors, including cooking time, method, and temperature. While some alcohol will always remain, the amount is typically not significant enough to make the dish alcoholic.

80. HOW DO MICROWAVE OVENS COOK FOOD?

Microwave ovens cook food by using microwave radiation to generate heat. The microwaves are absorbed by the food, which causes the water molecules in the food to vibrate rapidly, creating friction and generating heat. This heat is then transferred to the rest of the food, cooking it from the inside out.

Microwave ovens contain a magnetron, which generates the microwaves that are used to cook the food. The microwaves are directed into the oven cavity by a waveguide, and they bounce off the reflective metal walls of the oven, ensuring that the microwaves are evenly distributed throughout the food.

When food is placed in the microwave oven and the door is closed, the microwaves are turned on and pass through the food. The microwaves are absorbed by the food's water molecules, and as the water molecules vibrate, they generate heat. This heat then cooks the food.

It's important to note that not all materials are suitable for use in a microwave oven. Metals, for example, reflect the microwaves and can cause sparks or fires. Plastics can also melt or release harmful chemicals, so it's important to use microwave-safe containers and follow the manufacturer's instructions.

In addition to cooking food, microwave ovens are also commonly used to heat up drinks. This works in the same way as cooking food, with the microwaves being absorbed by the water molecules in the drink, causing them to vibrate and generating heat.

Out of interest... Microwave ovens are more energy-efficient than conventional electric ovens because they heat food more quickly and directly. In a conventional electric oven, the heating element heats up the air inside the oven, and the hot air then heats up the food. This process takes time and wastes energy, as some of the heat is lost to the environment.

In contrast, microwave ovens use microwave radiation to directly heat up the food's water molecules, causing them to vibrate and generate heat. This process is more efficient than heating up the air around the food, as it doesn't waste energy heating up the oven or surrounding air.

Another reason why microwave ovens are more energy-efficient is that they can be turned off instantly once the food is heated, while conventional electric ovens take longer to cool down and continue to use energy even after they have been turned off.

If you think it's because the Earth is closer to the Sun in summer, and further away in winter, you'll be surprised to learn that you're wrong! The weather is hotter in summer and colder in winter mostly because of the way the Earth tilts on its axis, and partly because of the Earth's orbit around the sun.

During the summer months, the Earth's northern hemisphere is tilted towards the sun, resulting in more direct sunlight and longer days. This means that the sunlight is spread over a smaller surface area, leading to more heating and warmer temperatures.

Conversely, during the winter months, the northern hemisphere is tilted away from the sun, resulting in less direct sunlight and shorter days. This means that the sunlight is spread over a larger surface area, leading to less heating and colder temperatures.

The Earth's orbit around the sun also plays a role in the changing seasons. The Earth's orbit is not a perfect circle, but rather an elliptical shape. This means that the distance between the Earth and the sun varies throughout the year. However, this variation in distance is not significant enough to cause the seasonal changes we observe.

Other factors, such as ocean currents and atmospheric circulation, also influence the weather patterns and temperatures experienced in different regions of the world. For example, ocean currents can transport warm water towards the poles, moderating temperatures in some regions. Atmospheric circulation can also cause air masses to move, bringing warmer or cooler air to different regions.

Bats are not blind, but they use echolocation (also known as SONAR) to navigate and hunt for prey. Echolocation is a system of using sound waves to locate objects and determine their distance and shape.

When a bat emits a high-pitched sound wave, it bounces off objects and returns to the bat's ears. The bat can then interpret the returning sound waves to determine the location, distance, and shape of objects in its environment. This allows bats to navigate through their environment and locate prey, even in complete darkness.

Other animals also use echolocation for navigation, including some species of whales, dolphins, and some birds. These animals emit sound waves that bounce off objects and return to the animal's ears, allowing them to locate prey and navigate through their environment.

Some animals also use other forms of navigation, such as magnetic fields or landmarks, to navigate through their environment. For example, some birds use the Earth's magnetic field to navigate during migration, while some ants use visual landmarks to navigate to their nest.

Birds use the Earth's magnetic field to navigate during migration. They have specialized cells in their eyes called "cryptochromes" that are sensitive to magnetic fields. These cryptochromes are believed to allow birds to "see" the Earth's magnetic field as a pattern of light and dark lines superimposed over their normal vision.

When a bird is exposed to the Earth's magnetic field, the cryptochrome cells in its eyes become aligned with the magnetic field lines. This alignment allows the bird to sense the direction and intensity of the magnetic field, which it can use to orient itself and navigate.

Research has shown that birds can detect variations in the Earth's magnetic field as small as 0.1% and can use this information to determine their position and direction of travel. They also use other cues such as the position of the sun and stars to navigate.

Scientists are still studying exactly how birds use the magnetic field to navigate and how they are able to detect such small variations in the field. However, it is clear that the ability to sense and use the Earth's magnetic field is a crucial part of bird navigation during migration.

Contrary to popular belief, cutting a common earthworm in half does not create two living worms. In most cases, the front part of the worm will survive and regenerate a new tail, while the back part will die. This is because earthworms have vital organs located in the front of their bodies.

However, there are some creatures that are capable of regenerating a complete body from a part that has been cut off.

One example is the starfish, which can regenerate an entire arm or even a whole new body from just a portion of its original body. This is possible because starfish have the ability to produce new cells and tissues to replace the missing ones.

Another example is the planarian flatworm, which can be cut into pieces and each piece will regenerate into a new, fully functional organism. Planarians have an exceptional ability to regenerate and are capable of regrowing entire heads, tails, and even brains.

So the ability of an organism to regenerate depends on its cell types and tissue structure. While some organisms have the ability to regenerate entire body parts, others may only be able to regenerate small portions or not at all. The process of regeneration is complex and is still not fully understood by scientists.

Interestingly, the common earthworm has several unusual biological characteristics that make it a unique creature. Some of these characteristics include:

- *Regeneration:* As mentioned earlier, earthworms have the ability to regenerate lost body parts. However, this ability is limited to the posterior end of the worm, as the anterior end contains vital organs that cannot be regenerated.

- *Hermaphroditism:* Earthworms are hermaphrodites, meaning they have both male and female reproductive organs. During mating, two earthworms will exchange sperm, allowing both to fertilize their eggs and produce offspring.

- *Multiple hearts:* Earthworms have multiple hearts, typically ranging from 5 to 10, depending on the species. These hearts pump blood through the worm's circulatory system, which is an open system that consists of a network of vessels and sinuses.

- *No lungs:* Earthworms do not have lungs but instead breathe through their skin. Their skin is moist and permeable, allowing oxygen to diffuse into their bodies and carbon dioxide to diffuse out.

- *Detritivores:* Earthworms are detritivores, which means they feed on decaying organic matter such as leaves, dead plants, and other debris. They play an important role in the ecosystem by breaking down this material and enriching the soil.

- *Segmented body:* Earthworms have a segmented body, which allows them to move through soil and burrow underground. Each segment contains muscles that contract and relax, enabling the worm to move in a wavelike motion.

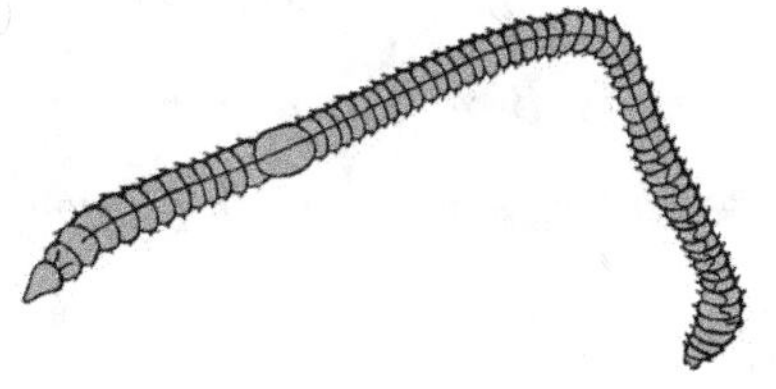

84. IF YOU PICK UP A BABY BIRD AND PUT IT IN ITS NEST, WILL ITS MOTHER DISOWN IT?

First, it is a common misconception that a mother bird will reject her young if they are touched by humans. However, this is usually not the case. Birds have a poor sense of smell, so they are not able to detect human scent on their young.

If you find a baby bird that has fallen out of its nest, the best thing to do is to try and return it to the nest. The mother bird will not reject the baby just because a human has touched it. In fact, the mother bird is more likely to abandon the baby if it is left on the ground, as it will be vulnerable to predators and the elements.

If you cannot find the nest or if the nest is too high to reach, you can create a makeshift nest using a small basket or container lined with soft materials such as grass, twigs, and leaves. Place the makeshift nest in a nearby tree or bush, as close to the original nest as possible. Monitor the baby bird from a distance to see if the mother bird returns to care for it. If the mother bird does not return within a few hours, you may need to contact a local wildlife rehabilitation center for assistance.

Remember that wild animals should be left alone as much as possible, and only rescued or handled by trained professionals!

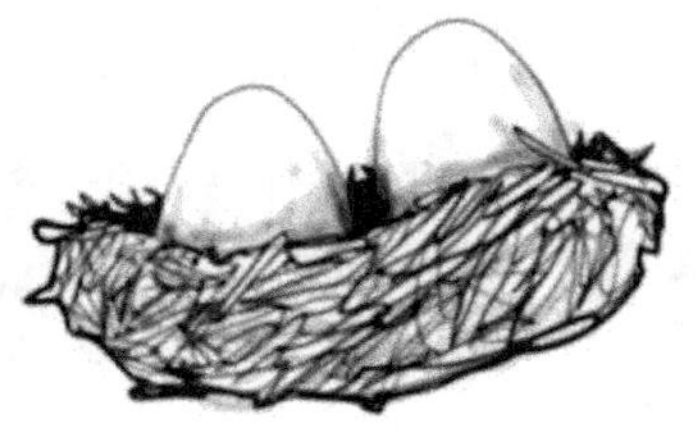

No, humans and dinosaurs did not coexist. Dinosaurs became extinct approximately 65 million years ago, while the first human-like species did not appear until around 2.8 million years ago.

Dinosaurs dominated the Earth for approximately 165 million years, until a mass extinction event occurred, likely caused by an asteroid impact. This event wiped out all non-avian dinosaurs and many other species, paving the way for the rise of mammals and birds.

The first true humans, Homo sapiens, appeared in Africa around 300,000 years ago, although the first members of the genus Homo appeared around 2.8 million years ago. Humans gradually evolved and spread across the globe, developing new technologies and societies as they went.

While humans did not coexist with dinosaurs, some modern animals, such as birds, are considered to be the direct descendants of certain dinosaur groups. For example, modern birds are thought to be descended from theropod dinosaurs, which include famous species such as Tyrannosaurus Rex and Velociraptor.

But you might have heard that the fossils of cavemen and dinosaurs have been found together in various places around the world. This is a common misconception perpetuated by popular culture, but it is not based on any scientific evidence. The last non-avian dinosaurs went extinct about 63 million years before the earliest known Homo species appeared on the planet. It's true that some of humankind's earliest ancestors, such as Australopithecus, did live alongside other animals which are now extinct (such as mammoths and saber-toothed cats) during the Pleistocene era, which ended around 11,700 years ago. However, these animals were still not dinosaurs.

No, not at all. The idea that shaving hair makes it grow back coarser and darker is a common myth. In reality, hair regrowth after shaving appears thicker and darker because the hair that grows back has a blunt tip, which can create the illusion of coarseness and darkness.

When a hair is shaved, the razor cuts off the top of the hair shaft, leaving behind a blunt tip. This blunt tip can make the hair feel thicker and more coarse than before. Additionally, since the shaved hair is shorter than the hair that was previously there, it may appear darker because it has not been exposed to as much sunlight or other environmental factors.

However, the idea that shaving actually changes the thickness, color, or texture of hair is false.

Hair growth is determined by factors such as genetics, hormones, and age, not by whether or not it has been shaved. In fact, shaving can actually make hair appear thinner over time, as the repeated cutting of the hair can eventually cause it to become weaker and more prone to breakage.

So, while shaving may create the illusion of coarser and darker hair, it does not actually change the hair's physical characteristics in any way.

87. DO YOUR FINGERNAILS REALLY CARRY ON GROWING AFTER YOU DIE?

The myth that fingernails continue to grow after a person dies has been around for centuries. However it is not true because the body's metabolic processes (including cell and nail growth) stop completely when you die.

The idea that fingernails continue to grow after death likely stems from the observation that the nails on a deceased person's fingers appear longer than when they were alive. This is due to the fact that the skin around the nails shrinks as it dries out, giving the appearance of longer nails.

In reality, fingernails are made up of dead skin cells that are pushed forward by new cells being produced at the base of the nail bed. Once a person dies, their body's metabolic processes stop, and no new cells are produced. Therefore, the nails cannot continue to grow.

It's important to note that although fingernails don't grow after death, they can give some indication of the time of death. Because the rate of nail growth is relatively constant, the length of a person's nails can be used to estimate the time since they died. However, this method is not very accurate and is usually only used in conjunction with other methods of determining time of death.

Warts are a common skin condition caused by a viral infection. It is not true that you can catch warts from toads. The bumps on toads' backs are not warts, but rather glands that secrete toxins as a defense mechanism.

Warts are caused by the human papillomavirus (HPV), which infects the outer layer of skin and causes the skin cells to grow rapidly, resulting in a small, raised bump. Warts can be spread from person to person through skin-to-skin contact or by touching objects that have been in contact with a wart.

The myth that warts can be caught from toads likely originated from the fact that toads secrete a toxic substance from their skin that can cause irritation or even skin burns if it comes into contact with human skin. This has led to the mistaken belief that toads can transmit warts to humans.

The bumps on toads' backs, also known as parotoid glands, are not warts. These glands secrete a toxic substance that serves as a defense mechanism against predators. When threatened, a toad will puff up its body and release this toxin, which can cause irritation or even death in some animals.

89. WHAT IS SLEEP-WALKING AND IS IT DANGEROUS TO WAKE A SLEEP-WALKER UP?

Sleepwalking is a disorder that causes people to walk or perform other activities while they are asleep. It is more common in children than adults, and tends to occur during the deep stages of sleep. It is generally considered safe to wake up a sleepwalker, although they may be disoriented and confused. In some cases, sleepwalking can be a sign of an underlying medical condition or mental health disorder, and treatment may be necessary.

Sleepwalking, also known as somnambulism, is a disorder of arousal that occurs during non-REM sleep, typically during the first third of the night. It is characterized by a person getting up and walking around while still asleep. The exact cause of sleepwalking is not known, but it is believed to be associated with a combination of genetic, environmental, and developmental factors.

It is generally considered safe to wake up a sleepwalker, although they may be disoriented and confused. Contrary to popular belief, waking a sleepwalker will not cause them to have a heart attack, go into shock, or die. However, it is important to approach a sleepwalker gently and calmly to avoid startling them, which could cause them to become agitated or even violent.

Sleepwalking is more common in children than adults, with up to 40% of children experiencing at least one episode of sleepwalking. It tends to run in families, and is more common in people who have other sleep disorders, such as sleep apnea or restless legs syndrome. In some cases, sleepwalking can be a sign of an underlying medical condition or mental health disorder, and treatment may be necessary.

But can sleep walkers actually see, feel, hear, touch and taste things while they're wandering around? Well, in a way, yes. They're in a state of altered consciousness where they are neither fully awake nor asleep. During sleepwalking, individuals may have their eyes open, but their vision is impaired, and their perception of reality is distorted. Sleepwalkers are often described as having a blank stare and may seem unresponsive to their surroundings. But they are definitely conscious enough to navigate their surroundings as they go.

Sleepwalkers do not have full awareness of their environment and are often unable to perceive sensations like touch and taste, and they may have difficulty hearing. In some cases, they may be able to feel pain, but this is not always the case. Overall, sleepwalkers do not experience the world around them in the same way as they would when fully awake.

No. The belief that it's dangerous to eat less than an hour before swimming is a myth.

When someone eats, blood is directed to the digestive system to help with the digestion process, which can temporarily reduce blood flow to the limbs. This can cause cramping in muscles during exercise, including swimming. However, this is only likely to happen if the person engages in strenuous exercise immediately after eating a large meal. Eating a small snack or light meal before swimming is unlikely to cause any harm.

This myth may have arisen due to a misunderstanding of the causes of cramps during swimming or other physical activities. It is important to stay hydrated while swimming and to avoid overexertion to prevent cramps and other health issues.

So why do muscles cramp during exercise? Muscles can cramp during exercise due to a variety of reasons such as dehydration, muscle fatigue, electrolyte imbalances, or overuse of the muscle. When a muscle cramps, it contracts involuntarily and may cause pain or discomfort.

Dehydration can cause an imbalance in the electrolytes such as sodium, potassium, and calcium, which are important for muscle function.

Muscle fatigue occurs when the muscle is tired and unable to relax properly, which can lead to cramping. Overuse of the muscle, particularly if it is not properly stretched and warmed up, can also lead to cramping.

In some cases, underlying medical conditions such as nerve disorders, circulation problems, or hormonal imbalances can contribute to muscle cramps during exercise.

So, regardless of how recently you ate before you go swimming, it's actually proper hydration, warm-up exercises, stretching, and adequate rest that help prevent muscle cramps during exercise.

The Coriolis Effect is a phenomenon that is often believed to determine the direction of water swirling down a drain or toilet. The idea is that this effect causes water to swirl clockwise or counter-clockwise depending on whether you are in the Northern or Southern Hemisphere. However, this is actually a myth, and the Coriolis Effect does not have any significant impact on the direction of water swirls in sinks, toilets, or any other small-scale systems.

Don't get me wrong, though. The *Coriolis Effect* **does** exist, and it occurs due to the rotation of the Earth. As the planet rotates, objects moving over the surface are deflected to the right in the Northern Hemisphere and to the left in the Southern Hemisphere. This is because the Earth's rotation creates an apparent force, known as the Coriolis force, that acts on moving objects. This force is responsible for many large-scale weather patterns, such as the rotation of cyclones and hurricanes.

However, the Coriolis Effect is a very weak force that only becomes significant over long distances and large time periods. In small-scale systems, such as sinks and toilets, other factors have a much greater impact on the direction of water swirls. The shape of the basin, the speed and direction of the incoming water, and any small disturbances in the water can all have an effect on the direction of the swirl.

The belief that the Coriolis Effect determines the direction of water swirls likely comes from a popular science experiment performed by the science presenter James Burke in the 1970s. Burke claimed that he had demonstrated the Coriolis Effect by observing water swirls in two bathtubs, one in the Northern Hemisphere and one in the Southern Hemisphere. However, it has since been shown that Burke's experiment was flawed and that the direction of the swirls was actually determined by other factors.

Despite the myth of the Coriolis Effect determining the direction of water swirls, there are actually several real-world examples where the Coriolis Effect does have a significant impact. As mentioned earlier, the Coriolis Effect is responsible for the rotation of large-scale weather systems, including hurricanes, typhoons, and cyclones. It also affects ocean currents, causing them to move in a circular pattern around the globe. In addition, the Coriolis Effect is used in a range of industries, including aerospace and navigation, where it is used to calculate the trajectories of moving objects.

So, while the Coriolis Effect is a real phenomenon that has a significant impact on large-scale weather patterns and ocean currents, it does not determine the direction of water swirls in sinks or toilets. The direction of water swirls in small-scale systems is influenced by other factors, such as the shape of the basin and any disturbances in the water.

No! The idea that aeroplane toilets flush waste out into the sky is a common myth. Aeroplanes actually store their toilet waste in tanks, which are emptied at designated facilities on the ground. While incidents of "blue ice" falling from the sky have occurred, measures are in place to prevent such incidents from happening and improve waste management systems.

Contrary to popular belief, aeroplane toilets do not simply flush waste out into the sky. In fact, most modern aeroplanes store their toilet waste in tanks that are emptied by ground crews at airports. These tanks are designed to be both secure and environmentally friendly, with measures in place to prevent leakage or spillage.

Aeroplanes use vacuum toilets, which operate

by sucking waste into a holding tank using a vacuum. This technology not only makes the system more efficient but also reduces the amount of water required to flush the toilet. Once the holding tank is full, it is emptied at a designated facility on the ground.

Despite the measures in place, there have been incidents of "blue ice" falling from the sky. This is frozen toilet waste that has either leaked from a holding tank or fallen from a plane's exterior plumbing system. While rare, these incidents can cause damage to property or injury to people below. In response to these incidents, aeroplane manufacturers and operators have improved their waste management systems and increased monitoring to prevent such incidents.

It's interesting to note that blue ice is not always blue - the color depends on what was flushed into the toilet waste. However, the term has become a popular way to refer to this phenomenon.

And what about toilets on trains? Don't those flush out onto the tracks? No! Another myth! Toilets on trains function similarly to regular toilets, but they require a more complex system to dispose of the waste while the train is in motion. Typically, trains have a holding tank that collects the waste from the toilets. The holding tank is located under the train and is designed to be easily removable, which allows for safe and sanitary disposal of the waste at designated locations.

The waste from the toilet is flushed into the holding tank using a vacuum system, which is connected to the toilet bowl. When the toilet is flushed, a vacuum is created that pulls the waste down into the tank. This is similar to the way that aircraft toilets work.

To prevent odors and other issues, the holding tank is often treated with chemicals or other products that break down the waste and help to reduce the amount of methane gas produced by the decomposition of organic matter. The tank may also be cleaned regularly to prevent blockages and other issues.

Some modern trains are equipped with more

advanced toilet systems that use less water and are designed to be more environmentally friendly. These systems may use composting toilets, which break down the waste using natural processes and do not require the use of chemicals or other treatments. Composting toilets are often used in remote or off-grid locations where traditional sewer systems are not available.

93. IS THERE REALLY A 'DARK SIDE OF THE MOON' THAT CAN'T BE SEEN FROM EARTH?

Yes, there is a dark side of the Moon (but it's not permanently dark). And because the Moon rotates around in the same amount of time as it does to orbit the Earth, we only see one side of it, the opposite of which is the 'Far Side of the Moon'.

The Moon's rotation and orbit are somewhat unusual compared to other objects in our solar system. The Moon does rotate on its axis, but it rotates at the same rate that it orbits Earth. This means that the same side of the Moon is always facing Earth.

As the Moon orbits Earth, it also rotates around its axis. The side of the Moon that is facing Earth experiences a gravitational force that keeps it facing Earth. This is called synchronous rotation, and it's why we only see one side of the Moon from Earth.

The side of the Moon that is facing away from Earth is sometimes called the "dark side of the Moon", but this is a bit misleading. While it's true that we can't see that side of the Moon from Earth, it's not permanently dark. The Moon still receives sunlight on its far side, just like it does on its near side.

NASA's Apollo missions, which sent humans to the Moon, were able to observe and study the far side of the Moon. In fact, they found that the far side has a different composition than the near side, with very much fewer large, dark plains.

So, while the Moon does have a "dark side" that we can't see from Earth, it's not permanently dark, and the Moon does rotate on its axis. Its rotation is just synchronized with its orbit in such a way that we only ever see one side of it.

94. HOW DO SPACE-WALKING ASTRONAUTS KNOW WHICH WAY IS 'UP' OR 'DOWN'?

Spacewalking, also known as Extravehicular Activity (EVA), is a critical component of space exploration, allowing astronauts to perform maintenance, repairs, and scientific experiments outside the confines of their spacecraft. However, performing tasks while floating in the vacuum of space can be disorienting, and one of the key challenges is determining which way is up and which way is down.

One of the primary ways astronauts orient themselves in space is through visual cues, which can be somewhat limited in the emptiness of space. However, the Earth is a prominent and recognizable landmark that is always present in the background, providing a clear point of reference. Astronauts can use their position relative to the Earth to determine which way is "down" and which way is "up."

Additionally, the International Space Station (ISS) is equipped with a number of orientation systems that help astronauts maintain their bearings. The station is equipped with a system of lights that provide visual cues to help astronauts orient themselves. These lights can be adjusted to create a horizon line, making it easier to determine which way is up and which way is down.

Astronauts are also equipped with a number of tools to help them orient themselves in space. One of the most important tools is the Simplified Aid for EVA Rescue (SAFER), which is essentially a small jetpack that allows astronauts to maneuver in space. The SAFER is equipped with a number of thrusters that can be used to adjust the astronaut's position and orientation as needed.

Another important tool for spacewalking astronauts is the Tethered Umbilical System (TUS). This system is essentially a long cable that connects the astronaut to the spacecraft, providing a physical connection that can be used to help maintain orientation. The TUS also provides power and communication links, allowing astronauts to communicate with the spacecraft and receive guidance as needed.

In addition to visual cues and orientation systems, astronauts also rely on their own bodies to maintain orientation. The human vestibular system, which is responsible for maintaining balance and spatial orientation, continues to function in space. Astronauts can use this system to help maintain their bearings while performing tasks in the weightless environment of space.

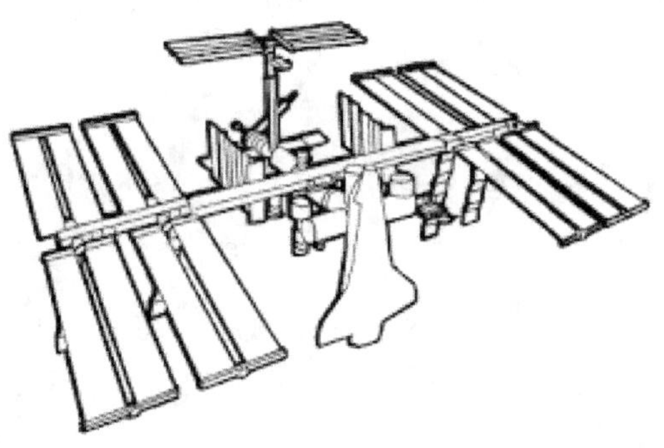

Mixing colored paints and colored lights follow different rules because they are based on different underlying principles. When mixing paints, the primary colors are red, blue, and yellow, which can be combined to create secondary colors, while mixing lights uses red, green, and blue as primary colors, which can be combined to create secondary colors.

The process of mixing colors is a fundamental aspect of art and design. However, the rules for mixing colors depend on the type of medium being used - colored paints or colored lights. The reason for this difference is because they are based on different principles of light and color.

Mixing colored paints is based on the

subtractive color model. In this model, each color represents the absorption of specific wavelengths of light. The primary colors in this model are red, blue, and yellow. When these colors are mixed together, they can create secondary colors such as orange, green, and purple. For example, when mixing red and blue paint, the resulting color is purple, which appears because the paint is absorbing both the red and blue wavelengths of light, leaving only the purple wavelengths to be reflected back to the viewer.

On the other hand, mixing colored lights is based on the additive color model. In this model, each color represents the addition of specific wavelengths of light. The primary colors in this model are red, green, and blue. When these colors are mixed together, they can create secondary colors such as yellow, magenta, and cyan. For example, when red and green lights are mixed, the resulting color is yellow, which appears because the light is adding both the red and green wavelengths of light, resulting in the yellow color.

The difference between the subtractive and additive models is due to the way that light interacts with matter. In the subtractive model, the pigments in the paint absorb certain wavelengths of light, while in the additive model, the colors are created by adding different wavelengths of light together. This difference in underlying principles means that the rules for mixing colors in these two mediums are fundamentally different.

96. WHY DO SOME THINGS FLOAT IN WATER WHILE OTHER THINGS SINK?

Why do some things float in water while other things sink? The reason for this phenomenon can be explained by the concept of buoyancy, which is the ability of an object to float in a fluid. The buoyant force acting on an object is equal to the weight of the fluid displaced by the object. If the object is less dense than the fluid, it will float; if it is more dense, it will sink.

When we say something is "less dense," we mean that it has less mass per unit volume. Conversely, something is "more dense" when it has more mass per unit volume.

Density is an important factor that determines whether an object will float or sink in a fluid. The density of an object is determined by its mass and its volume. For example, a rock is more dense than water because it has more mass in the same volume than water.

Another factor that affects buoyancy is the shape of the object. An object with a larger surface area will displace more water than an object with a smaller surface area. This means that a large, flat object may float even if it is more dense than water because it can displace a large amount of water.

The position of the center of mass of an object also plays a role in determining whether it will float or sink. If the center of mass is above the waterline, the object will tend to sink; if it is below the waterline, the object will tend to float.

Air trapped inside an object can also affect its buoyancy. For example, a helium balloon floats in air because helium is less dense than air. Similarly, a ship can float in water because it has a large amount of air trapped in its hull, which reduces its overall density.

It's worth noting that the density of water also varies with temperature and salinity. Cold water is denser than warm water, and saltwater is denser than freshwater. These variations in density can affect the buoyancy of objects in water.

Iron is attracted to magnets due to its magnetic properties, which are caused by the arrangement of its electrons. Other metals such as Gold, Silver, and Copper do not have the same magnetic properties. Magnets work by creating a magnetic field that attracts certain materials.

The North Pole and South Pole of a magnet have opposite magnetic properties, and this determines how they interact with other magnets and magnetic materials.

Magnetism is a phenomenon that occurs when certain materials are able to produce a magnetic field. These materials are called ferromagnetic materials and include iron, nickel, and cobalt. When these materials are magnetized, they become surrounded by a magnetic field that attracts or repels other magnetic materials.

The reason why iron is attracted to magnets is due to its magnetic properties, which are caused by the arrangement of its electrons. Electrons are negatively charged particles that orbit the nucleus of an atom. In most materials, the electrons are arranged in pairs, with each electron having an opposite spin to its partner. In ferromagnetic materials such as iron, some of the electrons have unpaired spins, which creates a net magnetic moment.

Other metals such as Gold, Silver, and Copper do not have the same magnetic properties as iron. This is because the arrangement of their electrons does not result in a net magnetic moment.

Magnets work by creating a magnetic field that interacts with other magnetic materials. A magnet has two poles: a North Pole and a South Pole. These poles have opposite magnetic properties, with the North Pole being attracted to the South Pole of another magnet, while the North Pole of one magnet repels the

North Pole of another magnet. When a magnet is brought near a magnetic material, the magnetic field of the magnet exerts a force on the material. If the material is also magnetic, it will be either attracted or repelled by the magnet, depending on its orientation relative to the magnet's poles.

To identify which end of a magnet is the North Pole and which is the South Pole, there are a few simple methods. One way is to use a compass, which will always point towards the Earth's North Pole. If the North Pole of a magnet is brought near a compass, the needle will be attracted to the magnet's South Pole, indicating that the end of the magnet nearest the needle is the North Pole.

Another method is to use a second magnet. If the North Pole of one magnet is brought near the South Pole of another magnet, they will be attracted to each other. However, if the North Pole of one magnet is brought near the North Pole of another magnet, they will repel each other.

The terms Mass, Weight, and Volume are often used interchangeably, but they have different meanings in physics. Mass is a measure of the amount of matter in an object, weight is a measure of the force exerted on an object due to gravity, and volume is a measure of the amount of space an object occupies. While Mass is a scalar quantity, Weight is a vector quantity, and Volume is also a scalar quantity.

Mass, weight, and volume are three fundamental concepts in physics, and it is essential to understand the differences between them. Mass is the amount of matter in an object, and it is usually measured in grams or kilograms. It is a scalar quantity, which means that it has only a magnitude and no direction. An object's mass does not change, regardless of its location or the forces acting on it.

Weight, on the other hand, is a measure of the force exerted on an object due to gravity. The weight of an object depends on the object's mass and the gravitational force acting on it. The weight of an object is a vector quantity, which means that it has both magnitude and direction. The unit of weight is the Newton (N).

It is essential to understand that weight and mass are not the same things. While mass is a measure of the amount of matter in an object, weight is a measure of the force that acts on it due to gravity. For example, the mass of an object remains constant, but its weight varies depending on the location. The weight of an object on Earth is different from its weight on the Moon, where the gravitational force is weaker.

Volume, on the other hand, is a measure of the amount of space an object occupies. The volume of a rectangular object can be calculated by multiplying its length, width, and height. The unit of volume is the cubic meter (m^3) or cubic centimeter (cm^3).

The Doppler effect, also known as the Doppler shift, is the phenomenon that causes the pitch of a sound to change as the source of the sound moves closer or farther away from an observer. This effect is commonly observed with emergency vehicle sirens, as well as with trains, planes, and other moving objects that produce sound.

To understand the Doppler effect, it's helpful to think of sound waves as a series of compressions and rarefactions that travel through a medium, such as air or water. When a sound source is stationary, these waves radiate out in all directions at a constant frequency, creating a uniform pattern of compressions and rarefactions.

However, when the sound source is moving, the waves in front of it become compressed, or "bunched up," while the waves behind it become stretched out. This creates a noticeable difference in the frequency and wavelength of the sound waves that reach an observer.

For example, when an ambulance with a siren on approaches a stationary observer, the sound waves in front of the vehicle are compressed, resulting in a higher frequency and a higher pitch. As the ambulance passes by and moves away from the observer, the sound waves behind the vehicle are stretched out, resulting in a lower frequency and a lower pitch.

The same principle applies to other moving sound sources, such as airplanes and trains. In the case of airplanes, the Doppler effect is especially pronounced because the speed of sound changes with altitude and air pressure. This can cause a noticeable shift in pitch as the plane approaches and passes overhead.

It's worth noting that the Doppler effect also applies to light waves, not just sound waves. This is what causes the redshift and blueshift observed in astronomy, where the wavelengths of light emitted by distant galaxies appear to be stretched or compressed due to their motion relative to Earth.

100. WHY DON'T PLANTS AND FRUITS GROW IN YOUR STOMACH WHEN YOU EAT THEIR SEEDS?

The belief that plants and fruits can grow in the human digestive system is a myth. Seeds require specific conditions to germinate and grow, which are not present in the human stomach, and the digestive system is designed to break down food, not support plant growth. So, if you accidentally swallow a seed, don't worry, it will simply pass through your digestive system harmlessly.

The belief that plants and fruits can grow in the human digestive system is a misconception that has been around for a long time. This myth is often perpetuated by children's stories and urban legends. However, it is not possible for plants and fruits to grow inside the human stomach.

Firstly, seeds require specific conditions to germinate and grow, which are not present in the human digestive system. For instance, seeds need moisture, warmth, and sunlight to grow. However, the human stomach is an acidic environment with little to no light or moisture. Therefore, it is impossible for a seed to grow in these conditions.

Secondly, plants and fruits have evolved to have their seeds dispersed by animals through their digestive systems. The seeds of many fruits and plants are designed to survive the digestive process and be excreted in the animal's feces, where they can then grow into a new plant. However, the seeds are typically protected by a hard outer shell that prevents them from being damaged by the stomach acid.

Lastly, the digestive system is designed to break down and absorb food into the body, not to support plant growth. The stomach acids and enzymes in the digestive system are designed to break down food and extract nutrients for the body to use. There is no support for plant growth or reproduction in the digestive system.

101. DO CARROTS REALLY HELP YOU SEE BETTER IN THE DARK?

While carrots do contain certain nutrients that are beneficial for eye health, there is no evidence at all to suggest that they significantly improve your vision. In fact, this idea may have originated as a World War II propaganda campaign to explain how British pilots were able to shoot down German planes at night. The campaign claimed that the pilots had exceptional night vision due to their high intake of carrots, when in reality, they were using new radar technology.

That being said, carrots do contain important vitamins and minerals that are beneficial for overall health. One of these is vitamin A, which is essential for healthy eyesight. Vitamin A helps to protect the surface of the eye and is also involved in the formation of the pigment that allows us to see in low-light conditions. However, it is important to note that consuming excessive amounts of vitamin A can be harmful, so it is recommended to get it from a balanced diet rather than supplements.

Carrots are also a good source of fiber, which is important for digestive health, and potassium, which helps to regulate blood pressure. They also contain antioxidants such as beta-carotene and lutein, which can help to protect against cellular damage and reduce the risk of chronic diseases such as cancer and heart disease.

In addition to their health benefits, carrots are a versatile and tasty vegetable that can be enjoyed in a variety of dishes. They can be eaten raw as a snack, cooked as a side dish, or used as an ingredient in soups, stews, and salads. Carrots also come in a variety of colors, including orange, purple, and white, each with its own unique set of nutrients and health benefits.

So, while carrots may not improve night vision, they are a nutrient-rich vegetable that can provide a range of health benefits when consumed as part of a balanced diet.

Peter Clark is a successful author, copy writer, researcher, and puzzle enthusiast, and has always been fascinated by how everything around him works. From as early as 4 years old, he started asking the kind of questions that most parents can't (or don't want to) answer!

Since then he has been the editor of several business news journals around the world, written more than a hundred business, general knowledge and fiction books, as well as this book's prequel, *Ask The Boffins!*

He's even produced a series of online educational games and word puzzles at **ClarksGame.com** ... so he's glad you've joined him now on his latest quest for weird, strange and cool facts about life, the universe and everything!

www.ingramcontent.com/pod-product-compliance
Lightning Source LLC
Chambersburg PA
CBHW070651250726

48662CB00001B/73